A DAY IN TOLEDO

ISBN-84-400-5929-9

Dep. Legal B. 15.093 - XVI

P. RIERA VIDAL
INSPECTOR OF ELEMENTARY SCHOOLS
TRASLATION BY
KEITH E. ARNOLD

A DAY IN TOLEDO

(ILLUSTRATED ARTISTIC GUIDE)

12º EDITION

REVISED AND ENLARGED
BY
M. C. ENRIGHT

1973

TOLEDO

Contemplating TOLEDO from afar, bathed in tints of golden ochre, her houses piled up on her hills, scattered among them a score of Mudejar towers and the Gothic one one of the Cathedral, we realize the hold this town took upon «El Greco» when he arrived in Spain — a fascination which never left him to his dying day.

TOLEDO is a nest of Art and History; of Tradition and Legend, each stone a memory, some legend attached to each nook and corner of its narrow, hilly, tortuous estreets.

It is a natural stronghold, perched on seven hills on the banks of the Tagus which, before reaching this spot, has flown peacefully along is wide bed amidst broad fields, and now turns abruptly into a narrow pass between steep, rugged cliffs, forming a loop which encircles the city on three of its sides. Once past the town the river again sweeps peacefully along a broad bed amongst pleasant fields, as before. Each end of the loop formed is guarded by one of Toledo's famous *bridges :* that of *Atcántara,* to the East, and that of *St. Martin,* to the West.

NOTE. — Many of Toledo's most important buildings have on different occasions been seriously damaged: during the so-called War of Succession (1701 - 1714), during the French invasion by Napoleonic troops (1808 - 1810) and again during the late Civil War (1936 - 1939).

The northern side of the town — the only side not protected by the river and bounded by strong embattlements slopes down to the plain (the «Vega»).

TOLEDO had been the capital of the Peninsula under the Goths, the Moors and the Spanish sovereigns since 555 — over a thousand years. From here, in Spain's powerful last era, the destinies had been ruled of that *«Empire in which the sun never set»*...

Now the impression of grandeur and melancholy, of strength and silence, derived from a visit to this once proud « Imperial City » is a deep and lasting one.

FOREWORD

Former editions of this booklet were prefaced by a report of the «Royal Academy of Fine Arts» in Madrid and of a Dedication», neither of them of interest for the foreign visitor to Toledo. Instead of these, notes have been added (pp. 8-15) that will, it is hoped, help to a fuller appreciation of what he is about to see.

The present edition has also been planned in a way that visitors may find as much information, in as abbreviated a form as possible; and the approach to the town (whether by car or by train) has also been taken into consideration.

PRACTICAL NOTES

VISITORS COMING BY TRAIN will find buses at the station rather distant from the city, which will take them to Zocodover Square in the centre of the town. On the way there they will have glimpsed the ruins of the Palace of

Galiana, in the plain; the mediaeval Castle of San Servando crowning a hill overlooking the river; the Alcantara Bridge spanning the Tagus where the river begins to narrow. Then the road, taking a sharp turn, passes at the foot of the beautiful Gate of the Sun, and from there into the town.

VISITORS COMING BY CAR from the Madrid road will, from quite a distance, see the old town perched on a height, outlined against the sky. Still on the outskirts of the city on the left, a large modern building (near-replica of Santo Domingo el Real which we shall latter see) is a factory of so-called «Damaskeened» work — typical gold and steel Toledo industry since the time of the Arabs.

A little further on, to the right, they will see the large dome of the Church of St. John the Baptist which forms part of the complex known as the Hospital of Tavera (pp. 16-18) where, if possible our first stop should be before entering the town itself.

ITINERARY FOR ONE DAY[1]

* * *

The office of Management of TOURISM (Oficina de Turismo) is situated in Zocodover Square, in the centre of the town.

TICKETS for visiting the buildings are to be got at the places themselves or — in a couple of instances — in a shop nearby.

_____

(1) A short visit will probably not allow for more than for visiting the places marked in this Itinerary in large print. However, other places of interest near-by or on the way there are given too, in smaller print.

HISTORICAL NOTES

The history of Toledo is as old as the hills upon which it rests. Many successive races have left their imprint upon it. It is known that Phoenicians, Carthagenians and Greeks traded with it from the earliest ages. As well as these, Romans, Visigoths, Arabs and Jews all mingled with the Celtiberians — the original people of the Península.

B. C. 193   The first historical fact, however is that given in the Roman Annals telling of their conquest of the « well fortied town » where they stablish a « colonia » with its citadel, forum, temples, baths, circus, aqueduct, etc. (p. 89). Though the remains of these buildings are but faintly traceable, they testify to its importance at the time.

A. D. 414   The Vandals sweep over the Spanish Peninsula devastating it. The Visigoths, crossing

A. D. 466   the Pyrenees threw them out and establish their own sumptuous capital in Toledo. Their court, a centre of learning and culture, is centre also of the Christian world of the time : in their Basilicas were held the first Synods and Councils (400-702). The history of Toledo then becomes the history of Spain.

A. D. 711   Hordes of Islam cross over from Africa. The Spaniards and Goths who can escape take refuge in the mountains of Asturias — and it is from here that the reconquest of their own country was to start which only ended centuries later (711-1492).

The constant riots at the beginning of the Mahomedan dominion are followed by a brilliant era : arts, crafts, science and letters flourish.

Moorish rule declined, just as had the Visigothic before it, and the descendants of those Spaniards who had in 711 fled to the mountainous North and had been since then step by step, regaining their own, stood before Toledo, led by Alphons VI of Castille and his A. D. 1085 famous warrior «El Cid». After a seven year's siege, they entered Toledo triumphantly. Moslem rule was at an end

» 1200 The Jews who, at times favoured, at times persecuted, had always loomed large in the annals of Toledo, became very powerful at this time. Their « Great Synagogue » (later Santa Maria la Blanca) was then built.

» 1350 The reign of King Peter I. — « the Cruel » — seethes with great internal strifes and disturbances. At his marked favoritism of tbe Jews, the nobles, rallying round his half-brother Henry of Trastamara, win the day and entering the city massacre the Jews and kill the King.

» 1368 Trastamaras from then on rule Spain.

To this Trastamara dynasty belonged Isabella of Castille and Leon who, through her » 1469 marriage to Ferdinand of Aragon, Catalonia,

Sicily, Naples, etc., united all these realms and provinces under one sceptre.

A. D. 1476   Battle of Toro gained by the partisan of Isabella over those of Princess Johanna, supposed daughter of Henry IV, nick-named « La Beltraneja », upheld by the Portuguese King. This Victory assures Isabella's succession on the throne and marks the beginning of Spain's « Golden Era ».

»   1492   This date in the reign of these Sovereigns known as the « Catholic Kings », marks the final driving away of the Moors back to Africa, the expulsion of the Jews, and the discovery of America by Columbus under the auspices of the great Spanish Queen, with Spanish means and Spanish ships manned by Spaniards.

»   1502   Queen Isabella's daughter Joan «the Mad» and her husband Philip « the Handsome » — (a Hapsburg, son of the Emperor Maximilian) — are proclaimed sovereigns of Spain and, through Philip, of the Netherlands. Philip

»   1506   dies young and Joan, insane, is locked up in a
»   *1516   castle, her father Ferdinand becoming Regent until Charles, son of Joan and Philip, takes possession of his great inheritance.

»   1566   Death of Charles I of Spain (since 1516) and V of Germany (since 1519).

»   1560   Philip II, son and successor of Charles V soon leaves Toledo and establishes his Court in Madrid, until then a small provincial town. It is the end of the splendour of Toledo.

11

ARTS AND STYLES AT THEIR DIFFERENT AGES

PREHISTORIC   Objects found in Toledo and its province can be seen in the ARCHEOLOGICAL MUSEUM (p. 36).

R O M A N   Of the important buildings known to have been built by the Romans 2.000 years ago in the «Vega» (p. 89) only faint traces are left: the so-called *Hercules Cave*, some stones and part of the arch of an aqueduct near the Bridge of Alcantara (p. 31) are the only remains of that period.

VISIGOTHIC   The Visigothic Kings lived in splendour, in magnificent buildings (the Aula-Regis, or King's Palace; the Atrii of the Nobles; etc.). The famous «Treasure of Guarrazan», of marked Bizantine character, tells of the luxury of the rule which ended with Roderick, their last King (p. 86). Of the buildings of the period only part of the city walls have survived and fragments of friezes, capitels, etc., whic can be seen in the ARCHEOLOGICAL MUSEUM (p. 36).

A R A B I C   This style is characterized by horse - shoe
a) Moorish shaped arches numerous columns and profuse ornamental motifs. We are told of fantastic palace, of curious hydraulic apparatus, of water clocks of intricate machinery. Nothing of this and only part of very few Monuments has survived (pp. 23-88).

b) Mudejar   This style, of which Toledo offers innumerable examples, appears *after* the Conquest of the Moors by the Christians. The conquerors, constantly on the battle-field around Toledo itself or in the south of Spain (still in Arab possession) it was the Moors—many of whom had remained in Toledo — who went on building for both their Christian conquerors and for the Jews, no builders themselves. The magnificent *Gate of the Sun* (Puerta del Sol); the *Castle of San Servando;* the *Bridges of Alcantara* and *St. Martin;* the «*Casa de Mesa*»; «*Taller del Moro*»; church of *Santiago del Arrabal,* most of the church towers, etc , are examples of it.

We are struck by the many churches of this time being a mixture of Christian and Sarracene spirit. On the other hand the beautiful « *Chief Synagogue* » (now Sta. María la Blanca) evidently the work of the Moors for the Jews — built also at this period (1200 ?) is in pure Arabic style. However, the *Synagogue* of Samuel Levi (1355)— now « *El Transito* », is Mudejar in its later period of Andalouisian influence : its friezes, pierced windows and polilobulled arches show the most exquisite workmanship of Moorish hands.

* * *

The Moorish character of architecture penetrated even into parts of the Cathedral in spite of the *Gothic* style from the North having been purposely adopted for this most important structure that was to be entirely free from Moslem influence.

G O T H I C   During two and-a-half centuries (1226-1493) arts, wealth, energies centred in the great CATHEDRAL. Artists of renown from the whole of Europe were proud to take part in it (pp. 42-46).

Though much of the work in this superb construction was evidently by Moorish hands, (triforium, doorway of the Chapter-Hall. Gudiel's Tomb. St. Eugene Chapel), yet it is pure Christian art — the first instance, in Toledo, of a complete break with the Moslem tradition dominant for so many years.

In this CATEDRAL, one of the most magnificent and interesting in the world, the evolution of the *Gothic* and of the styles which followed it can be well studied (p. 44).

RENAISSANCE   Most of the buildings after this are splendid
(Plateresque)   examples of *late Gothic* (St. John of the Kings) of *Renaissance* or *Plateresque* styles (the latter receiving its name from its resemblance to the work of the silversmiths (plateros) renowned in Spain at the time, such as the doorway of Santa Cruz and others.

The imposing Ñew Visagra Gate, the Alcazar, the façade of the Town Hall, the tomb of Cardinal Mendoza in the Main Chapel of the Cathedral, and several of the entrances of the same, doorways of churches and convents and many reredos belong to the so-called « *Second Renaissance* », More austere and simpler than the «First», and influenced by Greek and Roman ideals, it is typical of the buildings of the time of Charles V and his successors.

BARROQUE (Churrigueresque) This style often took in Spain a special form called «Churrigueresco», after the architect who introduced this modality. A striking example of it is the famous «Transparente» (p. 62) in the Cathedral.

NEO-CLASSICAL Then, once more the classical form predominates: façade of the Institute, Puerta Llana of the Cathedral, Arms Factory, and many doorways, reredos, etc.

* * *

Hospital of Tavera (XVIth. Century)

This building, known also as the « Outside Hospital » (de Afuera), or of ST. JOHN THE BAPTIST (1541), as well as a charitable institution is, as a writer has termed it, « a small Escorial » : palace, museum, temple and crypt, all in one.

The imposing, massive structure is due to the great Cardinal Tavera, of the powerful ducal Houses of Medinaceli and Lerma, still existant. He was the founder of this charitable institution for the destitute sick.

The architect Bustamante was entrusted with the plans of the building and many were the artists of the time — Spain's « Golden Age » — who took part in it, among others : Berruguete, Covarrubias, the Vergaras, Villalpando and Greco himself — not only as a painter but as sculptor and architect. Part of the building was to be a PALACE, the Cardinal being a great magnate of his time, chief Counsellor to the Emperor Charles Vth and ruler of the country during his master's absences

Entering the vestibule with its almost flat vaulted roof, a few steps on the left lead to a door opening into the magnificent rooms that once gave hospitality to many crowned Heads and Princes. Antique furniture, silver, valuable mirrors, tapestries, embossed coloured leather; Persian and Turkish rugs as well as old Spanish ones of Alcaraz and Cuenca, lamps, braziers, etc., and a splendid collection of paintings form an exquisite synthesis of the mansion of a « Spanish Grandee ».

Among the paintings of the Museum some of Greco's masterpieces are to be seen : the portrait, of Cardinal

Tavera; the beautiful « Holy Family »; the Baptism of Jesus (one of Greco's last works), St. Francis and « The Tears of St. Peter» and also by that same artist is a small sculpture of «Christ Resurrected». Other important paintings are: Titian's portrait of « Charles V at Mühlberg » (similar to that in the Prado Museum of Madrid) paintings by Carreño, Sanchez Coello, Lucas Jordan, Tintoretto, M. de Voos, Paul de Bryl, Salvatore Rossa, Caravaggio, and many others, as well, as a charming *primitive* by the « Master of Bruxelles ».

From the dining room a few steps lead down to the Archive, a nave of magnificent proportions, full of Mudejar parchmentbound books, historical letters and manuscripts of great value, — some set into recesses of the six-foot-thick walls.

Returning to the vestibule we pass to a spacious, imposing double courtyard with elegant columns. A portal by Berruguete forms the entrance to the church at the end of the central gallery. This CHURCH makes an impression of grandeur not easy to forget. A great octagonal dome is raised above the groin; the light flows from it in all directions; in the centre, the magnificent tomb of Cardinal Tavera by Berruguete.

Under the church, down steps hewn in the very rock, is the imposing CRYPT.

The part of the building destined to HOSPITAL formerly for the destitute sick has since the Civil War (1936-39), been turned Into a model orphanage and another part has free schools for needy children, under the patronage of the present Dowager Duchess and the devoted care of the Sisters of Charity of St. Vincent of Paul.

Attached to this charitable Institution is the historical, quaint XVI th century PHARMACY which gives the impression of an old alchemist's of by-gone days. Under oil lamps hanging from the ceiling are mortars, weights, measures, boxes finely docorated, blown glass, old Talavera jars, utensils, curious apothecary's books of the time, and a XVII th century lavishly decorated cupboard with innumerable small drawers and niches marked with the names of all kinds of herbs, potions, poisons (!) and precious stones to which, finely ground, great curative values were assigned. This curious PHARMACY was destined to the use of the sick of the Hospital. To-day, all related to charitable purposes is most modern and up-to-date.

* * *

Leaving Tavera, a broad avenue bordering a small park leads to the present entrance io the city . the magnificent NEW VISAGRA GATE (see next page) a finer approach to the old town than that of any other city.

The New Visagra Gate (XVI th Century)
(Puerta Nueva de Visagra)

This Gate, the pyramidal spires of which from a distance looks like enormous pencils with sharpened points, consists of two buildings, separated by a square courtyard. The sides of this courtyard are bound by high walls and are crowned by strong embattlements.

As yet we have not entered the Gate. We are standing before the front part of the building over which loom the two towers with their graceful spires.

As we walk under the arches of the dark roof we notice that most of these arches betray their Arabic origin and that the repairs in some very ancient doors denote the ravages of time. This Gate was restored thanks to the solicitude of a great king, the Emperor Charles V, in 1550 by the architect Covarrubias.

Let us now enter the square courtyard whose walls are crowned by stout battlements

Let us look at the arch we have just passed in order to admire a great coat-of-arms of Charles V, a double-headed eagle, worked in stone, against a background of red. We shall see this coat-of-arms in a number of places, principally in the Alcazar.

Under the coat-of-arms we see several small stones eagles, as if about to take flight. Above, loom the spires of the towers.

The other part of the building now in front of us, consists of a — semicircular — half pointed arch which gracefully outlines a background of green.

Above the keystone of the arch, set in a niche, is a small statue in white marble. It represents St. Eugene, first Archbishop of Toledo the story of whose martyrdom we shall see in the frescoes of the Cloisters of the Cathedral. This sculpture is attributed to the famous artist Berruguete. Having passed the half-pointed arch we can see an enormous and superb coat-of-arms of Charles V beautifully carved in rough stone.

On both sides are large round towers in which as if encrusted in them two statues of Visigothic kings complete the majesty and beauty of the New Visagra Gate. A Guardian Angel of stone lends a worthy finishing touch to it.

The Ãrab walls, restored by Alphons VI after he reconquered the City from the Moors (1085) are now opened up to allow for modern traffic.

Just passing through this Gate we come face to face with a graceful Mudejar — late Moorish — doorway and the Ãbsiss of SANTIÃGO DEL ARRABAL.

Santiago del Arrabal (XII th Century)

This church, one of the oldest in Toledo, almost as old as the Puerta del Sol was built shortly after the reconquest of the city by Ãlphons VI (1085). In its construction the remains of the Arab walls were utilized as may be seen if we look at the construction of the lower half of the tower. Several *ajimeces* (Moorish windows) clearly tell us so.

Besides these « ajimeces », the form of construction so frequent of the Toledan Ãrabs—alternate bands of masonry and brick — the windows of the bell-tower, those of the church walls (now bricked up to the left) and a series of beautiful arches which can be seen in the apses further down the street, tell us, too, of its Arabic construction.

Inside the building, towards the left, facing the Main Altar, the pulpit attracts our attention. It is of very beautiful Mudejar work. From this pulpit St. Vicente Ferrer, who is represented by the statue, excited the fervour of the Christian multitudes whit his famous sermons five centuries ago.

Panoramic view of Toledo

This Circumventing Road (Carretera de Circunvalación) which joins the bridges of Alcantara and St. Martin offers the most beautiful panorama that can be imagined. It is impossible to describe the impression and the emotion which it produces, from all points of this highway and specially from the terrace of the hermitage of the romantic « *Virgin of the Valley* » (Virgen del Valle). It would be unpardonable not to discover and enjoy the beauty of Toledo from this vantage point, the only spot from which a full panoramic view of this peerless city is to be had.

IMPORTANT NOTICE

Not far from SANTIAGO DEL ARRABAL, south east of the GATE OF THE SUN (Puerta del Sol) a road branches out, downhill, leading to the bridge and on to the CIRCUM-VENTING ROAD on the opposite banck of the river. The road is in excellent condition. Consulting the map of Toledo at the end of this booklet, it will be seen where the road begins (near PUERTA DEL SOL), forming a sharp corner. Here a large poster indicates the direction to follow. The road itself, running parallel to the river is marked only where it passes the bridges (that of ALCANTARA at one end, that of ST. MARTIN at the other). One may drive along the whole loop formed by the river, re-entering the town over the latter bridge and through the CAMBRON GATE (in which case it is practical to follow the visit of the city by the Church of ST. JOHN OF THE KINGS, fhe SYNAGOGUES, GRECO'S HOUSE and MUSEUM, etc.), or driving from ALCANTARA BRIDGE as far only as the before mentioned « VIRGIN OF THE VALLEY » and back again to the starting point, coming face to face to the strikingly beautiful GATE OF THE SUN (Puerta del Sol) and from there on as indicated in the following pages.

The Gate of the Sun (XII th Century)
(Puerta del Sol)

Though the exact date of its construction is not kown, it is certaintly the work of Moorish hands in its later Mudejar period when, as a conquered race the Moors who still remained under Christian rule worked for their conquerors.

This Gate, as most of the buildings of the time, partakes more or less of the character of fortifications : Alphons VI who, after over six years, siege had conquered the town in 1085, had still a precarious hold on it. The gateway provides an entrance between two walls : the inner, much older one, dates back to the Visigothic King Wamba (672-80); the lower, outer one, having been built in the time of Alphons VI after his re-conquering the city from the Moors (1085).

Of exceeding quaintness and majesty, this gateway forms a high tower with two flanking turrets : one square, butting on the inner wall, the other rounded, finishing off the later «enceinte». The portal is composed of six succesive arches, all in the Arabian horse-shoe shape. The outer ones, more pointed, are in pure Mudejar (later) style. Above the outermost arch is a double row of arcades of brickwork, gracefully intersecting one another.

On the second arch is a medallion in relief representing the Virgin offering the chasuble to St. Ildephons (a motive frequent in Toledo). Another relief in marble is supposed to represent the summary punishment of a dignitary of the town by King Ferdinand « the Saint », for having wronged two young women who applied to him for justice.

The battlements are of a type common enough in Spanish-Christian architecture but which, according to Mr. Street, may have been originally derived from the Moors.

When looking at this Gate we cannot but agree with Mr. O'Shea who writes : « The Gate, with its warm orange tints, that contrast so admirably with lapis-lazuli azure of the cloudless sky, its battlements fringing the top and opening vistas of most noble aspect, is a treasure for an artist ».

Gate of Valmardon (VIIth Century)
(Puerta de Valmardón)

This ancient gateway, the oldest remaining one of the many which, piercing its fortifications used to give entrance to the city, dates back to Wamba (672-80), great King of the Goths, who also built the old wall.

Accustomed as one's eyes get in Toledo to the many ornaments and the horse-shoe arches of the Arab architecture, one is here struck by the contrast of the rough, rather crude character of the former Visigothic period, of which this is one of the very few examples which, surviving so many vicisitudes, have come down to our times still in good state of preservation.

From this Gate, going up a steep street, we get another splendid view of the magnificent PUERTA DEL SOL (The Gate of the Sun). We then come to the ancient mosque of Bib-el-Mardon, now known as « THE CHRIST OF THE LIGHT ».

« The Christ of the Light » (X th Century)
(Cristo de la Luz)

This elegant and delightful little mosque was built by the Arabs about 980, on the site of a former Visigothic (Chistian) church — about 550 — known then as « THE CHRIST OF THE CROSS » of wich nothing remains but some shafts and capitals of rather crude workmanship.

What is left of the mosque is only a small part of what it once was; though, as some writers say, probably it was all on a small scale always.

Let us enter the solitary courtyard, which is full of memories. Over some trees loom the embattlements of the *Puerta del Sol.* A simple well presents to us its curbs, a memory of the ablutions of the Moors in fulfillment of their religious practices.

We will easily distinguish the two parts of the building, constructed in different epochs.

The first, which faces the street, is purely Arab, as can be seen by the horse-shoe shape of its doors, the blind arches overhead which cross one another in graceful manner (like those of the *Puerta del Sol*), the fretted lozenges seen further up and the brickwork inscriptions of verses from the Koran.

The other part of the building is Mudejar (later Arabic style).

This is expressed in its slightly pointed horse-shoe arches, some of which are stalactites, like those we have just seen in the upper part of the *Puerta del Sol* and in the apses of Santiago del Arrabal.

Probably that this mosque was at one time a Visigothic church. It is almost certain that three of the four columns in its interior belong to the ancient church, although it is also said that they may have formed part of the Basillca St. Leocadia. The fourth, as is easily seen is an imitation of recent construction.

Once inside the building it is necessary to look upwards, in order to contemplate the upper part of the mosque. In its small domes with ther beautiful ribbing, in its short arches, sustained by smalls columns of marble, the simple grandure of Arabic architecture is evident,

Climbing some steps we arrive at the Mudejar apse, on the walls of which we con distinguish some almost oblite-rated paintings of marked Byzantine influence, probably dating from about the close of the XII th Century when the building was remodelled into a Christian place of worship, the apse having been constructed two centuries later, when plans for the building of the magnificent Cathedral had already been made. Later restorations have been carried out when the ravages of time have made it necessary.

* * *

This mosque is perfumed with legends. Among those which are told, perhaps the one which has lingered most in the minds of the populace, through the years and the centuries, is as follows :

Il has been told from generation to generation that when Alphons VI entered Toledo in triumph on May 25 th 1085, together with the much-famed warrior known as « El Cid », his horse knelt down as it passed this building. One is even shown the stone on which the horse of the Leonese king bent its knee : the white stone on which we step as we enter.

Considering this a miracle, all was searched and, tearing down the masonry, a crucifix was found lighted by the feeble rays of a Visigothic lamp. It had been hidden there, the legend says, to avoid profanation when the arabs took possession of the capital, some years after having entered on Spanish soil. And there the crucifix remained with the lamp still alight, as a symbol that the light of the Christian faith would continue to inspire the conquered race during the 365 years of Moorish domination in Toledo. It is probably for this reason that this Moorish mosque is now called he HERMITAGE OF THE LIGHT.

A tradition also exists that the conquering Christian army first heard Mass there upon entering Toledo, and that, as the cross was missing, the shield of Alphons VI, served in its stead at the celebration of this religious service. We can see this shield when we visit the *Provincial Museum in the Hospital of the Holy Cross* (Hospital de Santa Cruz).

Again facing the GATE OF THE SUN after the detour to the GATE OF VALMARDON and to the CHRIST OF THE LIGHT, and going uphill, we come upon the so-called « MIRADERO » (which means a vantagepoint for looking out).

* * *

The «Miradero» Promenade
(or Terrace), and Banks of the Tagus

A magnificent view spreads before this lofty and spacious Terrace at the foot of which the river, coming from the mountains of Aragon, winds peacefully through the broad fertile valley extending between Aran'uez and Toledo, here encircling the old city.

On our left, almost at bird's eye view, we can see the NEW VISAGRA GATE. Further in the distance the large grey dome of TAVERA and the picturesque suburbs of ANTEQUERUELA or EL ARRABAL, protected by the outer wall and stretching down to the orchards banking the river. In the distance the bare hills of typical red earth of Toledo slope down, in striking contrast to the luscious green of the river banks. On our right the ruins of the PALACE OF GALIANA and the RAILWAY STATION are to be seen (the latter, a modern imitation of the Moorish style so typical of Toledo). Still further to the right the CASTLE OF SAN SERVANDO outlined, crowning a bare hill, keeps guard over the great ALCANTARA BRIDGE, the eastern access to the, then, great capital of the realm. Quite to the right, the new MILITARY ACADEMY is now being bu'lt, as the ALCAZAR, were the Academy housed in latter times, was destroyed in 1936 during the last Spanish Civil War.

* * *

It is said that in was in this immense «VEGA» (plain), at the foot of the « MIRADERO » TERRACE or PROMENADE, that, in the time of Alphons VIII, the Kings and Princes

27

of Navarre, Aragon, Vizcaya, Portugal, France, Italy and Germany, with their armies, rallied to take part in a Crusade — spurred on by Pope Innocent III — against the powers of Islam, which were routed by the Christian armies in the battle of Navas de Tolosa (1212).

Old annals tell of the grandeur and richness of the buildings which during the domination of the Goths spread over the part of the city between the high « MIRADERO » and the HOSPITAL DE SANTA CRUZ : of the Aula Regis (the Palace of the Gothic Kings) with all its treasures; of the Atrii of the Nobles, of palaces, churches, basilicas, etc., etc. In SANTA MARIA DE ALFICEM were held the first *Synods* and *Councils* of Christendom and in S. S. PETER and PAUL which, according to Menéndez Pidal seems to have been the royal pantheon, were suspended the so-called *« Votive Crowns»* of gold and precious stones which form part of the famous « TREASURE OF GUARRAZAN » where it had been buried and has been found after many centuries.

The Palace of Galiana

Between the emerald green of the fertile orchards, lulled by the eternal song of the Tagus, beyond the station, some ruins are to be discerned.

They speak to us of those far-off days, when the gentle Galiana only daughter of King Galafre, « the most beautiful Moorish lady of Moorish lands », who was wooed by Abenzaide, King of Guadalajara, whom she did not love and by Charles, later known in history as «Charlemagne» (?) son of the King of France whom she loved with passionate devotion.

The legend says that in the courtyard of this castle, on moonlit nights the gleams of the swords of the gallants shine like flashes of lightning in the fight which was to decide who was to be the husband of the Moorish princess, « the most beautiful Moorish lady of Moorish lands ».

And one still seems to hear, enwrapped in the murmur of the river, Galiana's cry of joy when she saw the French prince triumph over the Moorish king.

It is said that an aura of sadness fell over the palace as the happy couple went away to France, and that, because of this, grief is smouldering little by little throughout the centuries the legendary Palace of Galiana.

* * *

This palace is now crumbling into ruins in the midst of green orchards and broad fertile fields stretching to the edge of the river.

Traces of fine Moorish work, some tiling and arabesques still tell of this splendid palace of romantic reminiscences.

This spot was known after the re-conquest of Toledo (1085) as *La Huerta del Rey*, it being the King's property. About 1200 Alphons VIII had it repaired in its former luxurious Arab style for Rachel, the beautiful Jewess (« La Fermosa ») of whom he was deeply enamoured and it was here, during an absence of the Kings's that she met her tragic end. Many are the writers whom this theme has inspired. We next hear that at the end of the XIVth of beginning of XVth Century the palace became the property of the great Guzman family that added its coat-of-arms to the late Empress Eugénie, the beautiful Spanish wife of Napoleon III.

* * *

On the opposite bank of the river, high up en a barren hill, stands the CASTLE OF SAN SERVANDO overlooking the ample « Vega » (plain); at its foot the BRIDGE OF ALCANTARA which spans the river where it narrows and its banks begin to rise and close up on it, and forms the loop which encircles the city on three of its sides : east, south and west. (See map at end of booklet).

The Castle of San Servando (IX th Century)

This characteristic specimen of Mediaeval stronghold, crowning the height overlooking Alcantara Bridge, was built on the site of the Monastery which Alphons VI put in charge of the Monks of St. Benedict of Sahagún and Cluny, after his conquest of Toledo from the Moors (1086).

But the Monks, repeatedly attacked by the Arabs who were still fighting to reconquer the City, abandoned the Monastery. It was then made into a fortress and later bestowed by Alphons VIII to the Knights Templars that the they might defend the bridge and thus, the entrance to the city. At the suppression of the Order (1212) the castle fell into ruins but it was rebuilt, about 1385 by Archbishop Tenorio, keeping its old characteristics. Windows and arches exhibit Mudejar (late Moorish) influence.

In the large courtyard inside the castle and in another on its northern side can be seen the remains of Roman sepulchres hewn in the rock. It had probably been a cemetery in those by-gone days.

At the foot of the hill we see the famous ALCANTARA BRIDGE.

Bridge of Alcantara (IXth-Xth-XIIIth Centuries)
(Puente de Alcántara)

This celebrated bridge belongs to all epochs and is to be considered as much the work of the Christian as of the Moor.

The Arab structure (866-975) was built on the site of former Roman and Gothic constructions — as is to be seen from some stones, blocks and masonry near by. It was swept away in a great flood in 1257.

The then reigning monarch, Alphons X, « the Wise », had it reconstructed immediatly, that Toledo might not be cut off from the other towns. All that had been left of the bridge were the bastions on the banks, and one of the towers — a solid pile founded on the rocks. The great central arch and a smaller one were then built as well as a fortified tower at the outer (or country) end, which was replaced in 1817 by the present one. The majestic, hexagonal tower on the town side, with its picturesque turrets (about 1259) was again restored in 1489.

Strong and graceful it stands, were the — as far as here— wide bed of the Tajo suddenly narrows; where the pleasant green expanses bordering it abruptly become steep, barren hills and scraggy sombre rocks, where the peacefully flowing waters turn into swift current, caught between the mountains that rise from its sides.

Calvert's words about this bridge, come to our minds : ....« a noble bridge, old as the city — the work all Toledo's rulers and, like Toledo grim, stern rude, destined it would seem to endure forever. Romans, Visigoths, Moors, Castilians have lingered on it, triumphed on it, fought upon it, and across it today must walk every traveller entering with reverence this great temple of the mediaeval and bygone ».

* * *

Traffic is not allowed on this bridge any longer. All goes over the NEW BRIDGE, some yards further down stream.

Square of Zocodover
(Plaza de Zocodover)

This square is a true home of history. Here it was that the Arabs held their market — « Zoco » — in which were sold the finest products of the East : silks from Damascus, tapestries from India, spices from Malaya and from Ceylon....

The traditional market is still held each Tuesday, in which are to be seen the women of the town of Vargas who, seated gracefully with legs crossed and with their typical costume, evoke the memory of the ancient Muslin zoco (1).

It is reputed that it was in this square that the Castilian language was first spoken.

------

(1) At this traditional market still held on Tuesdays, it is not frequent any longer to see the costumes of old times.

Here is was that the townsfolk gathered for their popular feasts; here, too, tournaments were held, « Autos de Fe » during the Inquisition; here justice was meted.

It is also said that under an arch in its eastern side the most typical of the square, King Ferdinand « the Saint » used to listen from his throne to the complaints of his subjects, dispensing a serene but severe justice. We have already spoken in the PUERTA DEL SOL of the justice which was accorded to those maidens who complained to the king, because they had been wronged by the Governor of the city (p. 22).

Under the same arch King Ferdinand « the Catholic » proclaimed his daughter, doña Juana la Loca (Joan « the Mad ») and her husband Felipe el Hermoso (Philip « the Handsome »), King and Queen of Spain.

It this square, too, those who were condemned to death were executed. They were consoled in their last moments by the Brothers of the Cofradía de la Sangre (Confraternity of Blood). It is for this reason that the Cristo de la Sangre (The Christ of Blood) has in front of it a small altar lighted by a lantern which lends palid tints to its countenance of grief.

For the same reason the horse-shoe arch which outlines the background of rocks at the foot of which the Tagus flows is called « de la Sangre » and the inn of which we shall speak later is called « de la Sangre » too (p. 36).

Above the arch is the seat of the Government of the Province, a clock in its centre. All this part of the square was destroyed during the late Civil War (1936) but has since been rebuilt exactly the same as it was before. In the southeast corner, high above it, soars the top of the now reconstructed ALCAZAR (p. 37) flanked by its towers, as of yore. It, too, had been reduced to ruins in 1936.

But before visiting THE ALCAZAR we shall pass under the graceful horse-shoe arch « de la Sangre » and, going down some wide stone steps come upon the beautiful façade of the HOSPITAL DE SANTA CRUZ.

Hospital of the Holy Cross (1)
beginning of XVIth Century

(Hospital de la Santa Cruz) 1494-1514

Facing the heights crowned by the ALCAZAR this superb building was erected on the site of a former Arab palace and, prior to this, a Visigothic one.

It is due to the generosity of Cardinal Mendoza, private Counsellor to Queen Isabella. His thoughts, heart and wealth were all given to charity and he was the founder of this refuge for foundlings. This great man, dying in 1485, was unable to see commencement of his work. But in accordance with the terms of his will the Queen, who was its executrix, chose the site on which it wds to be built.

Nor was the great Queen able to see it finished because she, too, died in 1504, shortly after the great work and been commenced, and the architect Enrique Egas did not finish it until ten years later, in 1514.

---

(1) This building, skilfully and completly repaired, was an adequate frame to the magnificent exhibition « Charles V, and his Time » held in Oct. 1958 Feb. 1959. Historical and artistic treasures from the different countries which were the domain of Spain in her « Golden Era » were here brought together.

Here, as in all early specimens of Spanish-Renaissance architecture, the groundwork of the building appears to be the Gothic; the new ideas in the decoration and carving, exquisitely chiselled reliefs — as in this superb portal — enhancing its charm. The « Plateresque » windows are characteristic of the form this epoch developed in Spain.

Standing in front of the beautiful and famous doorway and, passing under the half-pointed arch, let us enter the vestibule of this fine building.

Several statues seem to be guardians of the entrance to it, to-day silent and empty.

We enter its spacious halls, built in the form of a Greek cross that is to say, with upper and lower parts of equal length.

Above the centre of this cross an imposing and graceful octagonal dome spreads the light. The angles and arches are profusely decorated and that the balcony also is a beautiful example of Renaissance work.

The lofty ceilings are of exquisite woodwork, the lower floor in Renaissance, the upper in Moorish style of great variety; the ample aisles right above one another on both floors, leave a large free space where they cross, a space soaring up to the very top of the dome, the whole forming an imposing structure.

During the Civil War (1936) the dome was destroyed and the whole building heavily damaged; but it has in these years been carefully repaired, regaining its former splendour.

* * *

In this same building (Hospital de Santa Cruz) is :

The Archeological Museum

It is reached through a doorway at the right-hand corner of the large entrance vestibule, which leads to the charming courtyards, full of silences and of memories, and to the rooms where archeological remains found in Toledo and its province are to be seen.

It is an interesting collection of prehistoric, neolythic, Ibero-Roman, Roman, Jewish, Visigothic, Arabic, Mudejar, Gothic objects and many others of historical or artistic value and interest too numerous to detail.

The splendid Plateresque staircase leading from the first courtyard to the upper story is of great beauty — as is, too, the Arab and Plateresque panelling.

Inn of the Blood or of the Sevillano (XVIIth Century)

(Posada de la Sangre o del Sevillano)

Opposite the Hospital of St. Cruz and the foot of the Alcazar, we find the famous « Inn of the Sevillano », also known as the « Inn of the Blood ».

A typical inn of the latter part of the XVIth and the beginning of the XVIIth Century it kept almost completely the character of the epoch until 1936, when it was destroyed during the late Civil War.

Cervantes, the world-renowned author of «Don Quijote» is said to have written here one of is famous novels.

It would seem that the spirit of the immortal genius who, in a small room of this typical inn, wrote while Greco near the «Tránsito» painted his marvellous paintings, lingers here still.

The Alcazar

This impressive structure, an imposing landmark of the city, stands on the highest point of Toledo.

It is difficult to say to what epoch it belongs, having gone through innumerable vicissitudes, reconstruction and radical transformations.

In Roman times a citadel (the «Arx»), it was also a stronghold during the Visigothic domain; was, we are told, a «fortified and impregnable place» in 1154, and was further restored and strengthened by succesive Castilians Kings — specially Alphons X «the Wise» (1253-84).

The Emperor Charles V, about 1538, ordered his great architect Covarrubias to rebuild entirely the rude, heterogenous mass it had become in the course of time. Many were the great artists of that age — Spain's « Golden Era » — who worked on it, the new construction being finished during the reign of Charles V's son and succesor Philip II. This King soon took the Court to Madrid and since then (1560) the rulers of Spain have never again lived in Toledo's Alcazar.

This fortress-palace has undergone many transformations: burnt down in the so-called «Succession War» of 1710, and restored; desfroyed by Napoleon's troops in 1810; burnt again in 1887 and destroyed during the late Spanish Civil

War 1936, and has now again rebuilt exactly the same as it was before the onslaught. It has been garrison post and partly prison, residence of Kings and Emperors; later, for a time, School of Arts and Crafts — Toledo having been renowned for its silk, wool and linen weavers, as well as many other industries. Since 1882 it became the site of the Royal Military Academy and was still fulfilling this purpose when the Civil War broke out (1936), when the Toledans who sided with General Franco's uprising made a heroic, well-nigh homeric resistance. They had meager weapons and less food; were attacked on all sides by the enemy, the huge building falling in ruins all around them, yet, like the old-time heroes of Sagunto and Numancia, without surrendering.

Its reconstruction is now (1961) nearly completed and it will be made into a Museum.

From its northern terrace is one of the finest views of Toledo.

The Military Academy which had formerly its seat here is now at its new quarters, in front of the old Alcazar, on a height on the opposite bank of the river.

On the way from the ALCAZAR to the CATHEDRAL, we pass the *Corral de Don Diego* and the *Prison of the Brotherhood* which follow here:

The Courtyard of Don Diego

(Corral de Don Diego)

This picturesque gateway gives entrance to a courtyard around which several houses are built.

Once inside, to the left, are some beautiful but badly preserved remains of a Hall decorated in Arabic style. It is now a workshop.

It is said that this, at one time, was the palace of King Henry II of Trastamara.

Prison of the Brotherhood

(Cárcel de la Hermandad)

Continuing downhill, and leaving on our left the Theatre of Rojas, in front of the later walls of the Cathedral, we are confronted suddenly with an ancient and beautiful Gothic gateway, and a superb coat-of-arms of Ferdinand and Isabella.

Those people who associated with the object of hunting down the evil doers enjoyed certain privileges and their association was called the *Hermandad* (Brotherhood). Hence the name given to the building.

Later, in it was held the Tribunal of the Inquisition.

The upper arch is ogival or Gothic. On each side of the shield we see a *cuadrillero*, one of those soldiers whose task it was to pursue the bandits who infected the uninhabited places and had their main haunts in the mountains of Toledo.

These *cuadrilleros* used to shut up their prisoners in caves which were completely dark and damp, as can still be seen in the cellars of the house — to-day an inn — and it seems that they applied very severe punishments of an inhuman nature, even to the point of immuring the criminals in the walls, if we are to go by the evidence of certain hollows we can see in the old walls.

* * *

Continuing on our journey southwards round the famous Cathedral, a few steps on, we reach the Square of San Justo with a church of the same name and, going through characteristic windings, we get to *San Juan de la Penitencia*.

San Juan de la Penitencia (XVIth Century)

This Franciscan Convent and Church adjoining were built by orders of Cardinal Cisneros (1514) and finished by the Bishop of Avila (1528).

Remains of the semi-Moorish palace of the Pantojas were utilized in its construction. The whole building bears traces of Mudejar workmanship but is a curious medley of styles: Arab, Gothic, Renaissance, Barroque and Plateresque. According to Amador de los Ríos this complex was undoubtedly still at that time (1845) «one of the richest in Toledo». During the late Civil War (1936) it wast mostly destroyed. Its exterior, in very simple Gothic style, is the only thing one can now see of it.

Just opposite these ruins and the picturesque absiss is the workshop of the living talented artist Julio Pascual to whom cne cf the beautiful « rejas » of the Cathedral (that in the Mozarabic Chapel) is due (See p. 45).

Back to the Cathedral, on its southern side we have the splendid *Gateway of the Lions* Further on is the so-called

Puerta Llana and opposite is the slope which leads to the street called «Of the Bitter Well» (Pozo Amargo) famous for the legend attached to it, (see «Legends» at the end of this booklet).

Turning the next corner of the Cathedral towards the west we come to the principal façade with its three great Porches and two towers.

At right angles to this marvellous front is the great Palace of the Cardinal-Archbishop with its pure Greco-Roman porch, such as this style was reborn in Spain.

At the other side of the Square, facing the Cathedral, is the *Town Hall*.

Town Hall (XVIIth Century)
(Ayuntamiento)

This simple and elegant building, slave to the plain contours of the Greco-Roman style, more austere and colder than the Gothic, is obviously in the same style as that which Herrera planned for the rear of the Alcazar and for the Escorial. It is said that the author of the plans for the building was George Theotokopulos, the son of El Greco.

The entrance to this building a broad stairway leads from the ample vestibule to the majestic Session Hall. The ceiling, painted in fresco, represents the four cardinal virtues with their attributes. The walls are covered with hangings of crimson velvet worked with magnificent designs of crowns, palms and other motifs, and the imperial eagles, with the arms of Toledo woven in the material itself : all of it the work of the once famous factories of this city, now disappeared. At the end of the room is the Chapel of the Town Hall, where formerly the Aldermen heard Mass before attending the sessions.

In the archives is a collection of decrees of no small historical importance, in view of the fact that they were the pattern on which were based those of Castille. We shall also see the banner of the city.

The Toledan Councils which, before this building was constructed (about the year 1614) had held their most important sessions in the cloisters of the Cathedral, were celebrated here thereafter.

At the back of the Town Hall (and belonging to it) is a quaint «Passage», closed during the night by iron gratings. In this Passage and in a large low-roofed old vault is a picturesque sale of antiquities.

And now, returning to the Cathedral, a few steps away, we stand before the imposing façade of the great Metropolitan Cathedral.

The Cathedral (1227-1497)

Of all the Monuments of Toledo, this building is the most important. « Sumptuous without gaudiness, austere without gloominess, it is one of the noblest specimens of Gothic architecture the world affords » (Calvert).

This edifice does not impress the foreigner as typically national corresponding, in fact, no longer to the temper of the nation. It was raised as a protest against the Moorish infuences which have passed into the life and art of Spain and without which nothing can be taken as representatively Spanish.

This was to be no longer the work of the infidel, but a new temple which should never have been contamined by Muslim rites, as was the case with Mosques that had been converted to Christian uses. King Ferdinand III «the Saint», and the Archbishop Don Rodrigo de Rada laid the first stone in 1227. The first architect was one *Petrus Petri* whose identity continues to be a matter of controversy. «This, at any rate», says G. E. Street, «is certain; whether French or Spanish, he was thoroughly well acquainted with the best French churches or he could not otherwise have done what he did». There was nothing in Spain then to lead gradually to the Gothic style. Even after the conquest of the Moors (1086), the latter continued to act as architects for Christian buildings, whether secular or ecclesiastical and, indeed, to monopolize all the art and science of the country which they no longer ruled.

One well understands that, although the Toledans may have been content to employ Mahomedan art in their ordinary works, yet, when it came to be a question of rebuilding their Cathedral on a scale vaster than anything which had as yet been attempted, they would be anxious to adopt some distinctly Christian form of art and lacking any school of their own in this respect, would be more likely to turn their eyes north to the neighbouring nation. However, in the triforium of the choir Moorish influence is still visible. (Calvert).

The names of many of the architects, — those between 1270 and 1425 — have been lost.

The succesive styles of architecture naturally influenced the original scheme. In 1493 the main structure of the stupendous fabric was completed. Some of the chapels were later additions.

This Cathedral is justly called the « MUSEUM CATHEDRAL » because of the many examples of all architectural styles which it contains : In its general construction the ogival or gothic prevails, as it does too in the windows, in many chapels and in a great part of the decoration. The plateresque-renaissance predominates in the greater part of the grilles and in a good many reredos. Greco-roman-renassance in the chapel of the «Sagrario», in one of the organs of the Choir, in several rededos and in the Sacristy. Granadine-arab in a tomb in the chapel of St. Eugene which we will visit later. Arab arches can be seen in the high part of the transept-in the triphorium. In the Main Chapel churrigueresque (Spanish baroque) in the so-called «Transparente» and finally the neoclassic in the Puerta Llana, outside.

During two and a half centuries the best artists of the world left the traces of their magic fingers, of their immortal creations in the Temple we are now going to see.

Here *sculpture* was ennobled to its highest by the technic of Berruguete and Borgoña, of Salvatierra and Covarrubias, of Vergara and Narciso Tomé. of Almonacid and Copín of Holland, of Rodrigo and Petit Jean.

Painting was raised to immortal rank by John of Burgundy, Caxes, Carducio, Lucas Jordan and Rizzi; the most famous pictures of the Greco, Tristan, Michel Angelo, Titian, Veronese, Tintoretto, Van Dyck, Bassano, Bellini, Rafael of

Urbino, Morales, Zurbarán, Goya, Velázquez, Guido Reni... rival in this insuperable jewel casket.

Wrought iron reached its highest art with Villalpando and Céspedes, John Frances and more recently, the grate-maker of Toledo, Julius Pascual who, in the silent Square of St. John of Penance works wonders of the metal in his hands.

The *stained glass*, shedding its golden gleam, and singing upon the altars its polychrome symphony, was the delicate and brilliant work of the famous glaziers Gusquiem of Utrecht, and Jacobo Delfin, of Peter Bonifacio, Friar Peter Cuesta Jiménez, Gonzalo of Córdoba, Nicolás Vergara and Master Henry of Toledo.

Among the finest features of this noble Church are ist eight principal entrances. In the western façade are the Portals — *Puerta del Perdón* in the centre —, flanked by the *Puerta de los Escribanos* and that of «*The Tower*», all dating from the first half of the XVth century.

The *Puerta del Perdón*, the principal one, forms a noble arch richly ornamented an divided into two smaller arches by a column surmounted by the figure of Christ above which are the Twelve Apostles. Above these a relief in Renaissance style represents the gift of the chasuble to San Ildefonso (a motive recurring frequently in Toledo). The smaller doors have single arches sculpted with statues of angels and patriarchs. Above the portals the façade is adorned with a colossal sculpture of the Last Supper. The façade is pierced by a beautiful rose window thirty feet across, with a glazed arcade beneath. On the south side are the *Puerta Llana*, in the classic style (1800), and that of «*the Lions*» which gives acces to the transept and is a magnificent Gothic work (1460).

It is a perfect structure: the six columns of the Ātrium are surmounted by six lions holding shields. Here are the famous bronze doors wrought by Villalpando and Ruy D. del Corral in 1545. The wood carving and decoration was the work of many masters. At the opposite, or north end of the transept, is the *Puerta del Reloj* (of The Clock) dating from the beginning of the XIVth century and so named from the clock above it. The door is of bronze and above it a fine rose-window of about the same period, considered by G. E. Street as the best example of stained glass now remaining in the Catedral [1]. Leading into the eastern cloister are the doors of *Santa Catalina* and of the *Presentation* (1565).

The cloisters are entered from the west side next to the Tower, by the *Puerta del Mollete*, so called because «molletes» or rolls were distributed to the poor here.

It is through this door that we enter the Cathedral [2] passing by the cloister, its centre full of greenery.

Lef us glance quickly at the frescoes painted by Bayeu and Maella, which represent scenes from the martyrdoms of the Saints, and then enter the sacred precints by the plateresque Gateway of the Presentation. Inside standing on the steps of the Porch of Pardon, the main porch, in order to better contemplate the interminable rows of columns — 88 of them — great vaults, and beautiful windows — there are 750 — and to take in at one glance the immense ensemble of the five naves, in the centre of which we find the Main Chapel and, as in all Spanish Cathedrals, the Choir.

(1) Many of these beautiful stained glass windows were destroyed during the Civil War (1936).

(2) The other doors are generally, if not always, closed.

In order to form a small idea of the artistic beauty of this monumental temple, let us visit one after the other the different chapels, overlooking those of lesser artistic interest.

Starting from the *Porch of Presentation*, by which we entered, we come on the right to the part in which is contained the *Great Treasure* of the Cathedral.

On the left, in front of the Chapel of doña Teresa de Aro, commonly called «*The Chapel of the Christ of the Spoons*» (notice the shield of its front) is to be seen, backing against a large column, the *Chapel of tho Descent*.

Chapel of the Descent

(Repaired in 1610)

In its the form of a huge tabernacle, and was built in order to commemorate the miraculous appearance on the same spot, in the year 666, of the Virgin to St. Ildephons, when she descended from Heaven to impose the chasuble on him.

This miraculous scene is represented very often in the Cathedral, in view of the fact that it his the motif of its principal Coat-of-Arms. It was sculptured on the rededos of this same chapel by Borgoña, the famous artist who carved part of the choir stalls, and left traces of his talent, as we shall see, in other parts of this Cathedral.

In this chapel the stone is venerated upon which, according to tradition, the Most Holy Mother of God set her feet when she descended from Heaven. It can be seen and touched through a small grille.

Returning towards the chapels, we shall see an altar placed against a wall: it is the altar of «Our Lady of Antigua».

Altar of « Our Lady of Antigua »

(XIVth Century)

The rededos, Gothic (or ogival), is of stone. The most interesting part is the figure of the Virgin with the Divine Infant in her arms, beause it seems that it was already venerated in the ancient Visigothic church which existed on the same site

Before the Virgin in front of us, were blessed the banners of the Christians who, on setting out to fight the Moors, swore to defend bravely their Fatherland and their Faith.

This image is very ancient. For this reason it is known as the « Virgen de la Antigua » (The Ancient Virgin).

The Chapel of the Baptistry

It has a Gothic doorway and a plateresque grille. The grille was made by Céspedes (1524), he who ruined himself in the construction of the wrought-iron grille of the Choir of this Cathedral.

In the centre of the chapel is to be seen the beautiful bronze baptismal font in plateresque style, admirably worked and bearing a curious picture (XVth to XVIth centuries).

After the *Chapel of Piety* (XVIth Century) which is the one following it, there is a picture on the wall representing St. Diego of Alcalá, worth studying from different angles.

Further on, after the Gothic porch of St. Catherine (end of the XIVth Century) is the Chapel of St. Peter.

Chapel of St. Peter

On the ojival Porch, amply adorned, are the bust of the Prelate who founded it — Don Sancho de Rojas (1420)—, the quiet figure of St. Peter, and fresco-painting by Bamontes, relating to the life of the Saint. The sculpture is attributed to Berruguete.

In the inner part is the canvas of Bayeu «The Healing of the paralytical ». In this Chapel—which is the Parish of the Cathedral — are buried its founder, Cardinal Inguanzo, and the humanist John of Vergara. There are other painting of Bayeu—brother-in-law of Goya—. The grille of the gateway belongs to the famous grate-maker John French (Juan Francés).

Equally magnificent are the four inside reredos, with their corinthian columns.

Immediately after, we find the *Porch of the Fair or of the Clock.*

Porch of the Fair or of the Clock
(XIIIth & XVIth centuries)

We will go outside for a moment in order to look at this porch.

It is gothic or ogival. Our attention is attracted by the great number of images of Saints, children, and angels, which decorate the arches and the tympanum. As may be seen, the sculpture is rather primitive. It is the fist time for many centuries that architecture and sculpture have been united, much to the surprise of the Mudejars, *who did not copy living being in their artistic works,* in accordance with the rules of the Arab style, *because they were prohibited by the Koran.*

The lower part is no less interesting. Above all, the doors are worthy of admiration; they contain very fine iron work covered with bronze (XVIIIth Century).

Worthy of note, too, are the groups of sculpture representing the Annuntiation and the Appearance of St. Leocadia to St. Ildephonse in the Basilica of St. Leocadia.

Amongst the canvases to be seen on either side, the most note worthy is that of the presentation of the plans of the Cathedral to King Ferdinand III, « the Saint », by Archbishop Jiménez de Rada.

* * *

Before continuing our visit of the chapels, we will stand for a moment between the *Main Chapel* and the *Choir* before we come to the line of seats, with our backs to the *Puerta del Reloj.* In front of us, further on, is the Puerta de los Leones (the Porch of the Lions).

The spectacle in front of us is a veritable orgy of art.

Never have the greatness of Art and of Faith become so interwoven as in this spot.

On our left the celebrated grille of the Main Chapel, in which iron, bronze and brass have interwined at the behest of a great artist : *Villalpando.*

On our right another grille sings the glory of yet another famous artist who has left on it the traces of his skill and his abnegation : *Céspedes.*

Both give entrance to artistic and religious treasures: the imposing and majestic *reredos* in which larchwood became as piable as wax in order that it might interpret the artistic conceptigns of Egas and of Borgoña; of Petit-Jean and of Copin of Holland; of Gumiel and Almonacid; and the famous choir stalls on which Berruguete and Borgoña worked in glorious competition...

In the background soars, solemn and magnificent, the most beautiful porch of the Cathedral : the Porch of Lions.

The vision of art is overwhelmingly beautiful. Light filters through several superb windows and through a beautifully carved rose-window and sheds over this magnificent scene the marvels of the rainbow.

Grille of Villalpando (XVIth Century)

It was worthy of a more solid and more beautiful setting than ordinary stone; for this reason jasper and marble were chosen.

On these materials is set the famous grille, with its bars of unsurpassed wrought-iron; beautiful caryatids and atlases support the first frieze. Above, other bars which become more and more rounded until they finish in another frieze enriched with beautiful heads in relief, cherubs and other motifs, worked with astounding perfection.

Between the columns are a number of balusters—a combination of candelabra — really delightful.

The second frieze terminates in shields, targets and torch-holders. In the centre of these the eagles of Charles V, the most powerful monarch of is time, spread their wings.

Above the proud eagles is raised the image of the Crucified One, a worthy and symbolic ending to one of the finest grilles which exist in the world.

* * *

The pulpits, solidly placed on two thick columns of marble, look like two enormous gaurdians of the ponderous grille.

The artist himself wrote the most modest of commentaries on this great work, in the most obscure corner of the famous grille : on the lowest part of the last bar, on our left, is written « Labor ubi cumque » (Here everything is work).

This said Villalpando, the famous craftsman who constructed this grille, the doors of the Porch of Lions and the majestic stairway of the Alcazar in the middle XVth Century.

Interior of the Main Chapel

(XIVth & XVth Centuries)

Its enormous rededos, a marvellous combination of delicate art and of great faith, is imposing. It represents scenes from the life, passion and death of Our Lord and is finished off by a splendid Calvary on a blue spangled background.

In this Chapel the famous artists Egas and Borgoña, Petit-Jean and Copin of Holland, Gumiel and Almonacid, Villalpando and others, lavished their skill and talents.

History his represented on both sides of the altar by the royal tombs of Alphonso VII, of Sancho III, « the Desired », and of Sancho IV «the Valliant», hanging like nests.

On our left, in a fine mausoleum, sleeps the famous Cardinal Mendoza, he who first waved the Christion standard from the Granadine tower, who lavished the greatness of his heart and dedicated the greater part of his wealth to the foundation of the *Hospital of Santa Cruz*, and who helped Columbus in his great enterprise of discovering the New World.

In his testament he expressed the wish that he should be buried in this honourable place. But to make this possible it was necessary to demolish the Gothic wall which was identical to the one opposite. The Chapter was resolutely opposed to this. Nevertheless Queen Isabella, who was the executrix of her confessor's testament, imposed her sovereign will and one night the pickaxe freed the space where to-day is erected the magnificent plateresque sepulchre where the great Cardinal rests in eternal sleep († 1495).

* * *

Further on near the reredos, we see, close together as if sharing the same glory, a shepherd and a King. The humble shepherd's crook close to the pompous regal crown. They represent the celebrated shepherd who guided the Christian army to victory at Navas de Tolosa, achieving in that place in the year 1212 a resounding triumph over the power of the Muslims.

In front of them on the opposite wall, there is a Moor and an Archbishop. The Moor represents the famous Kadir who, as a mediator of peace, saved Toledo from a day of mourning when it was reconquered by Alphonso VI. The Archbishop represents Jiménez de Rada, whom we saw in the *Porch of the Clock* presenting the plans of the Cathedral to King Ferdinand « the Saint ».

Above, a superb ceiling with a most beautiful nervature, bordered profusely in gold.

In the cellars under the Main Chapel the body of St. Ursula is kept in an ebony urn.

THE GRILLE OF CESPEDES (XVIIth Century) guards the entrance to the Choir. It is rather more simple than that of Villalpando, but is of no less merit or elegance.

The Choir (XV-XVIth Centuries)

Behind this magnificent grille by Cespedes is the famous Choir, with its celebrated double choir-stalls, its most elegant altar, its « *White Virgin*» whose countenance is illuminated by a peerless smile.

This Choir, its slender lecterns profusely adorned with gold, an enormous eagle, wings stiffly extended, its sumptuous organs; the figure of a kneeling cavalier Lope de Haro at the foof of the one on the left, under the trumpet of the angel which proclaims his fame, is unique.

Berruguete in the high Choir stalls on our left, and Borgoña on our right, lavish prodigally the treasures of their great talents in the most beautiful artistic competition.

Jasper, alabaster and walnut, all submitted the softness of their texture to the sublime caress of the fingers of those peerless sculptors.

The lower choir stalls carved fifty years earlier should not be overlooked. In them the style of the epoch was also marvellously employed by another artist Maestre Rodrigo. Each «picture» tells in wood of some victory of the Spaniards over the moors, in their inch-by-inch century-long reconquest of their of own land.

Above, the imposing group of the Transfiguration designed by Berruguete is a worthy finishing touch to the many marvels contained in the famous Choir of the Cathedral of Teledo.

We will now walk right round the outer part of the choir (XIVth Century), admiring the small altars of St. Mary Magdalene and of St. Isabella of Hungary; the marble columns which, it is said, belonged to the ancient mosque, and the frieze with its rough sculpture representing passages from the Holy Scriptures. In the space behind the choir, are the *Chapels of St. Catherine, Our Lady of the Star* (XVIth Century and of the *Recumbent Christ* (XVIIth Century); lovely sculptures attributed to Vergara, which symbolize Innocence and Guilt and a magnificent sculptural group which represents the Eternal Father and the Creation.

On the other side, the same marble colmuns, the same rough sculptures with scenes from the Holy Scriptures and the small altars of St. Michael and St. Stephen.

* * *

And now that we have walked right round the Choir let us return to the Porch to the Clock, in order that we may visit the Chapel of the «Sagrario».

Chapel of the Virgin of the Sagrario (or the Sanctuary)

(XVIth & XVIIth Centuries)

It is very ancient but was restored in greco-roman style by Cardinal Sandoval y Rojas, whose ashes are buriet at the left of the altar.

In this Chapel is venerated with extraordinary devotion the Virgin formerly known as St. Mary and which is now worshipped under the name of the Most Holy Virgen of the Sagrario or Sanctuary (XIIIth Century).

This figure is said to have belonged to the Apostles and to have been brought to Toledo by St. Eugene, its first Bishop.

It is also said that this venerable image dates from the time of the Goths, who hid it so that it should not be desecrated by the Moors, and that it was buried for over three centuries, until it was solemny restored to Christian worship when Alphonso VI reconquered Toledo (1085).

It is made almost entirely of silver, and on its mantle are a great number of pearls. But it is not for material value that it is venerated, but for its divine charms and miraculous power, which invite the visitor to go down on his knees and recite a Salve...

* * *

On leaving this Chapel we shall see on one of the tombstones a very modest incription : « Here lies dust, ashes, nothing »: It is the tomb of Cardinal Portocarre-ro († 1709) almost at the feet of all this pomp...

The Sacristy

Its beautiful hall is a veritable museum of paintings.

In front of the door by which we enter we see a magnificent corinthian altar, with exquisite marble and bronzes. Between its columns is one of the most attractive pictures by El Greco.

This canvas, to which two corinthian columns act as guards of honour, is the famous «Spolliation of Christ», that is to say, the dividing of His garments by the Jews.

In the antechamber of the Sacristy, there are two canvasses representing the « Torture of St. Andrew », by Vincent Carduccio and the «Martyrdom of St. Peter», by Eugene Caxés.

In the Sacristy, we must ben to the pictorial glory of lofty artists, among which overtops the Greco, with his famous «APOSTOLATE» (that is, the twelve Apostles), — a replica of which is in Greco's Musem. — We also admire here the picture of « St. Luke the evangelist » (said to be the self-portrait of the painter), «Jesus blessing», «The Tears of St. Peter, and, set in a magnificent rededos the famous «Spolliation», compendium of great beauty of the art of the Cretan painter. Herewith, the small sculptural group of the «Imposition of the Chasuble on St. Ildephonso», mo-delled by the same celebrated artist: one of the few examples of his work as a sculptor.

Moreover, there are in the Sacristy other paintings of universal great masters.

«The Appearance of St. Leocadia to St. Ildephonso», « The Birth of Jesus » and « The Adoration of the Kings», by

Orrente; «The Arrest of Christ», and the portrait of Cardinal Borbon, by Goya; «The Dolorosa», by L. Morales; «The Holy Family» (known as «The Pearl»), by Van Dyck; «The Flight to Egypt» by an unknown master: The dazzling ceiling was painted by Lucas Jordan. — The portrait of the famous painter himself looks out of the high windows.

The Ochavo (XVIth & XVIIth Centuries)

It communicates with the Sacristy. It is a hall, also in greco-roman style, and is called the Ochavo because it has eight sides.

It contains an immense quantity of relics related to Our Lord, to the Most Holy Virgin and to innumerable Saints.

It is, in addition, a veritable treasure house of art, represented by small chests and coffers, sculptures, urns, busts, crosses, etc.

Two great urns of hammered silver contain the remains of St. Eugene and of St. Leocadia.

Other reliquaries contain venerated mementoes of extraordinary interest for us: a piece of the veil of St. Leocadia, cut off by St. Ildephonse from the Toledan Virgin on the occasion of her miraculous appearance in the year 666; the knife which Recesvinto gave to the Saint in order that he might cut the veil; a thorn from the crown of Christ; a piece of the Holy Cross...

In addition, the famous standard which Cardinal Mendoza waved from the Granadine tower when this beautiful

Andalusian town was retaken from the Moors — 1492 —, the date of the discovery of America and of the finishing of the Cathedral.

We then pass to the *Vestry*.

Vestry

In the anteroom we are attracted by a beautiful roof painted by Claudio Coello and a collection of paintings by very famous painters :

«Portrait of Cardinal Borgia », by Velazquez.

«Virgin and Child » and « Jesus and the Samaritan », by Rubens.

«St. Francis », by Guernico.

«The Birth of Jesus» and the «Circumcision», by Bassano.

«St. Philip» and «St. Charles Borromeo», by Guido Reni.

«Baptism of Jesus », by Jordan.

«Portrait of Paul III », by Van Dyck,

«Burial of Jesus », by Bellini.

«Rossetes », by Mario Fiori.

«A Monk », by Zurbaran ...and many others.

A fresh motive for astonishment is provided by this sumptuous vestry. In it, besides many pictures of celebrated artist such as Titian, Greco, Rubens, Van Dyck, we find, carefully preserved in great show cases, very rich and historic religious vestments used by the Archbishops and Cardinals who have through many centuries occupied the Primatial, (or Metropolitan), See.

We can also admire some rich tapestries the most cele-brated among them being the « Tanto Monta » which belonged to King Ferdinand and Queen Isabella.

Let us not forget either the banners of the battles of the Salado (1340) and of Lepanto (1572).

We will leave by the same place we entered, passing the *Chapels of the Christ of the Column* and of. *St Leocadia* in order to enter the folloving :

Chapel of the New Kings (XVIth Century)

The « New Kings » are those of the family of Trastamara who ruled the destinies of Spain during the first seventy-five years of the XIth century, before Ferdinand and Isabella. The « Old Kings » are those who sleep their last sleep on both sides of the altar of the Main Chapel.

The entrance to this platererque Chapel is the work of Covarrubias, he who worked also on the Alcazar, on the Porch of Lions and in many other places. He was the architect of Charles V.

On entering this Chapel we are confronted by the tombs and recumbent statues of King Henry II, of his wife, Joan, of his son John I, of Henry III, and other royal persons.

Also the armour worn by the Portuguese Ensign Duarte de Almeida who, when fighting bravely against the Spanish forces in the battle of Toro (1476) having lost both arms was heroically defending his banner between his teeth when made a prisoners by soldiers of Ferdinand and Isabella.

The paintings in this Chapel are by Maella, the same artist who painted some of the francoes in the Cloister. The roof is very beautiful.

Chapel of Santiago or of D. Alvaro da Luna
(XVth Century)

This chapel, one of the largest and most beautiful in the Cathedral, is entirely in gothic or ogival style.

It was founded by the Constable Don Álvaro de Luna [1] as burial place for his family.

Don Alvaro, who was beheaded (1453) by order of King John II — is buried in the tomb on the right. His wife, Doña Juana of Pimentel (1488) in that on the left.

These admirable and severe tombs, in beautiful gothic style, are, in the centre of the Chapel. In the other sepulchres are buried a son, a brother and other members of the family.

In the lower part in the gothic rededos (1498), in the 2nd and 4th squares, the unfortunate couple are represented in an attitude of prayer.

High up on the walls are the shields of Luna and of Pimentel.

Here his the example of a man — Don Alvaro de Luna — who, from the steps of the throne, from which he had imposed his will, passed to the steps of the scaffold in Valladolid, in the middle of the XVth Century; some 20 years before Ferdinand and Isabella succeeded to the throne.

Chapel of St. Ildephonse (XVth Century)

Next to the Chapel of Santiago is the Chapel of St. Ildephonse. On the central arch at the entrance Narciso Tomé

---

(1) Below is the pantheon where his descendants are still buried. The present ones are the Duques of Infantado.

painted the portrait of Don Esteban Illan, he who proclaimed Alfonso VIII King of Castille from the Tower of St. Roman.

In this Chapel, which is also spacious and beautiful, Cardinal Albornoz, founder of the Spanish College of Bologna, Italy, is buried. His sepulchre is the one in the centre. It is handsome but rather ravaged by time. The other tombs are the burial places of persons of his family, amongst whom is the Bishop of Ávila.

Three architectural styles can be clearly discerned in this Chapel; ogival or gothic in the arches, ceiling, windows and in some of the tombs; plateresque in the tomb of the Bishop of Avila, on the right of the central reredos; and neo-classic in the central reredos, of the XVIIIth. Century, which represents the miracle of the Virgin putting the chasuble of St. Ildephonse in marble, jasper and bronze.

In front is to be seen that daring artistic feat known as « The Transparente ».

The Transparente
(middle of XVIIIth Century)

This altar, situated exactly behind the Main Chapel is called the «Transparente», owing to the fact that through an opening in the centre, light passes to the Sacrarium; light which in its turn comes from high up in a vaulted ceiling, opened up with great daring by the same architect who planned, painted and worked on this famous altar : Narciso Tomé, in 1732.

It belongs to the churrigueresque style of which it is one of the most admired and most discussed examples.

It has all the characteristics of that peculiar style : few straight lines, abundant curves incompfete and twisted columns, stone-work in imitation of flames, clouds and sea waves; many angels a great deal of protruding sculpture and and a sensation of artistic disorder and of exaggeration. Two atlasses sustain the masonry which serves as a niche for the Virgin and above, in the centre, a representation of the sun and its golden rays, the four archangels around it. Further up, in a hollow, the twelve Apostles with Our Lord; still higher, some beautiful sculptures representing Faith, Hope and Charity, the whole sorrounded by broken columns, plump angels, tongues of fire, curling waves and bronze plaques containing biblical scenes. At the sides are the images of St. Eugene and St. Leocadia, ond the left; of St. Ildeponse and St. Casilda on the right.

Almost the whole of the work is in Genoa marble.

It was finised in 1732.

* * *

Continuing our visit to the Chapels we will leave that of the *Holy Trinity*, which has a very fine grille, and that of *St. Nicolás,* which is very dark, in order to enter, the :

Chapter Hall (XVIth Century)

Its gothic porch is very beautiful and elegant.

The anteroom, square in shape and small, contains several cabinets which are of great merit, specially those on the left. The panelling of this anteroom, very brillant and fanciful, the work of Francis of Lara and James López Arena is mudejar.

The doorway which gives entrance to the Chapter Hall is Arab, with beautiful stucco work in colours.

Cardinal Cisneros, who also embellished the Main Chapel and founded the Mozarabic Chapel, ordered this Hall to be constructed. In his time also the famous Custody was made.

The architect who designed this chapel was Enrique Egas, the same of the Hospital of Santa Cruz (p. 34).

On the left and right of the anteroom several walnut lockers of beautiful Mudejar work of great merit serve as a frame to the door giving entrance to the Hall.

In this *Chapter Hall* the best work of the epoch is to be found : valuable frescoes by Borgoña, the celebrated artist whose work we admired in the Choir; some dazzlingly beautiful Mudejar panelling of shining gold and fast colouring. All arou d are the portraits of all the Archbishops who have occupied the Toledan See, painted by Borgoña up to the time of Cisneros; the portrait of Sandoval, by Tristan; that of Moscoso by Ricci; that of Inguanzo by Vincent López.

Same lovely choir stalls, the best being the plateresque, throne of the Archbishop, the work of Copin of Holland who also worked, as we already know, on the construction of the reredos of the Main Chapel. On this seat rests an ancient tablet, a *Gerard David*, of great merit and beauty representing the Virgin whith the Child in her arms.

* * *

At the side of the Chapter Hall is to be seen the *Chapel of St. Gil*, whose reredos is attributed to *Berruguete;* the *Chapel of St. John the Baptist* with a fine crucifix of ivory, of great artistic and symbolic value; the *Chapel of St. Anne*, whose plateresque grille is very elegant, and the *Chapel of the Old Kings.*

Chapel of the Old Kings (XVth Century)

The most notable part are the grille of its small choir — the one at the entrance —, by Cespedes (the artist who ruined himself by the grille of the Main Choir); the central reredos, which is plateresque, as is also the grille at the entrance, and a canvas of the Holy Countenance, with a barroque frame in the place of honour.

It is called the *Chapel of the Old Kings*, because it was here that the Chapel was transferred which held the remains of those Kings who for more than six centuries have slept their last sleep and of whom we spoke in the Main Chapel: Alphonso VII, Sancho III the Desired, and Sancho IV the Brave...

Next is the *Chapel of St. Joseph*. In is the picture representing St John, is attributed to Ribera (also knows as « El Españoleto »).

Now we are in front of the famous Porch of the Lions.

Porch of the Lions (XVth & XVIth Centuries)
(INNER VIEW)

We have already admired it when we had our backs to the Porch of the Clook. We can now look closely and enjoy its exquisite art.

In this porch the Gothic and Plateresque styles seem to compete in showing the marvels of which both are capable.

The Gothic style lavishes its filigree work on the outer portal and on the sides.

The plateresque spreads its charms, its delicaty, from top

to bottom, imprisoning the « processional » organ, as if wishing to play a hymn of triumph for its sovereign art.

This art achieves the purest style in the doors. One must get close to them in order to fully appreciate the beautiful carving of this work of the celebrated Villalpando.

A rose of light overhead appears to crown with glory this lavishness of art and talent.

Chapel of St. Eugene (XIVth Century)

It is one of the oldest in the Cathedral. In this Chapel three architectural styles can be clearly distinguished : the ogival or gothic in its grille and its windows; granadine-arab in a very beautiful tomb, covered in stucco lacework, which belongs to the founder of the Chapel, Gudiel; and plateresque in the tomb on the left.

The reredos too is very notable. It was designed by Enrique Egas, of the Hospital of Santa Cruz, was carved by Copin of Holland, who worked on the reredos of the Main Chapel, and was painted by the celebrated Borgoña, he who executed the choir stalls.

We come to the *Chapel of St. Martin*, of which the gothic grille and the plateresque reredos are interesting.

We then arrive at the *Puerta Llana*.

Puerta Llana (Plain Porch)

This is the only entrance-gate to the Cathedral which has no steps and for this reason is called the *Plain Porch*. It is the only style which was wanting to complete this temple besides the Arab, Mudejar, Gothic, Plateresque, Greco-Roman, and Churrigeresque styles.

Next is the *Chapel of the Conception*, with its grille and its reredos, also gothic, and that *of the Epiphany*, completely Gothic too.

Having pased the sloping tombs of the Archdeacons, we now arrive in front of the *Mozarabic Chapel*.

Mozarabic Chapel (XVIth Century)

It was founded by Cardinal Cisneros (1505).

By a special privilege from Rome this « Mozarabic Rite» had been admitted after the reconquest (1086), the Christians having been loyal to it, as inherited from the Visigoths, during the centuries of Moslim dominion.

Mass is celebrated in it every morning in accordance with these old Gothic rites different in form, in ceremony and in vestments from the usual ones. Special priests, called Mozarabic chaplains, are attached to it.

A Gothic or Ogival grille by John Frances (1524) with the shields of Cardinal Cisneros and paintings by Borgoña and above, the « Virgin of Anguish » give entrance to this chapel.

The interior is dazzling : outstanding is a picture by Borgoña representing the capture of Oran. On the altar is a Virgin in mosaic (XVIIIth Century) wich was for some time at the bottom of the sea, owing to the boat which carried in from Rome having been wrecked.

A Crucifix, made of a single piece of Mexican fennel is also of interest.

The Choir, surrounded by railings, is by the Toledan artist Julio Pascual (p. 40)

The ceiling is extraordinarily beautiful.

On leaving, let us think for a moment on the greatness of Cardinal *Cisneros* († 1517), the first novice of *San Juan de los Reyes*, Regent of the Kingdom, Conqueror of Oran. Founder oi the University of Alcala and he to whom this Cathedral owes its Main Altar the Great Monstrance, the Chapter Hall and the Chapel we have just visited.

* * *

Outside this chapel, is a small *Christ of Forgetfulness* (XVIth Century) at whose feet those who are suffering from grief caused by human forgetfulness come to pray and to weep; we see, too, the enormous Pascal Candle and, passing in front of the *Gate of Pardon*, we shall be confronted by the *Chapel of the Tower* where, behind the magnificent plateresque porch of Covarrubias, is kept the « *Great Treasure* » of the Cathedral.

The Treasure Chamber[1]

As we enter we are dazzled at the sight of so much gold and art, and so many marvels.

Here is kept the famous mostrance made by Heinrich Harfe (XVth Century) worked in part, it is said from the first gold which was brough from America by Columbus.

A wooden statue of great merit, representing St. Francis of Assisi by Peter of Mena.

---

[1] Most of the valuables in this room were stolen by the « Reds » during the late Civil War (1936-1939).

The four parts of the world, in spheres of silver besprinkled with precious stones.

An artistic silver tray, attributed to Benvenuto Cellini.

The mitre of Cardinal Cisneros.

The Golden Fleece which belonged to Charles II.

Breast-plate and ring belonging to Cardinal Gomá (1941); a silver palette, with which Cardinal Portocarrero closed the gateway of the Holy Year in Rome in 1700; a Virgin carved in box-wood (XVIIth Century); a chalice of silver and rock-crystal; a silver sphere besprinkled with rubies and diamonds weighing over 100 pounds, given by Doña Marianne of Neuburg, the window of Charles II. A silver tray representing the « Trial against Filotas », another one representing the « Rape of the Sabines » (XVIIth Century); a silver « manga » (or Cross) given by Cardinal Cisneros; a silver censer with relics of St. Leocadia given by Joan the Mad; a gothic sword, belonging, it is said, to Alphonso VI; another one given by our Generalissimo in 1939; silver trays, representing « The Sacrifice of Alexander »; and the « Death of Darius »; and many other jewels of insuperable historical or artistic value.

Amphors, jars, trays, miniatures, an interminable series of objects on which richness, luxury art and faith have left their imprint...

Let us take a final look at the great Temple, the pride of Toledo, the artistic glory of the race.

* * *

The Hall of Giants and the Great Bell

Entering the door opposite to that under the arch of the Palace and situated in the upper cloisters is the *Hall of Giants* which contains a number of grotesque figures, strangely dressed. Amongst these, the monstruous «Tarasca».

The «Great Bell», at the summit of the Tower, is 18 feet in circumference, nearly 12 feet high and weighs over 18 tons.

A magnificent view over Toledo is to be had from here.

* * *

Leaving the Cathedral and going uphill between the Archbishop's Palace and the Town Hall and through the Passage behind the latter we shall come to a magnificent gothic porch which belongs to the house known as of « the *Toledos* » in the wall of which, facing the Convent of the Ursulines, we can see a lovely *ajimez* or Moorish window. Under this ajimez an ancient cross spreads out is bare arms.

Once again we see gathered together in a small open space several architectural styles: the gothic in the door of «the Toledos», the arab in the «ajimez» of the same house and the mudejar on the outside of the Convent.

Straight on round the convent we see, in the apse, more arches and work in Mudejar style.

The street is deserted, nobody inhabits this ruined and lonely corner which leads us to the Street of Santo Tomé where, in the church of the same name, Greco's famous picture, «The Burial of Count Orgaz» is kept.

Santo Tomé (Street and church)

When we enter this street and leave the church of San Salvador on our left we see a beautiful, slender mudejar tower rise above the grey houses.

Between the bands of masory and brick, Visigothic stones stand out here and there similar to those we saw in the Bridge of Alcantara, in the walls of the city and in the Lane of St. Gines..

This tower belongs to the parrochial church of Santo Tomé the church which proudly preserves one of the most notable pictorial jewels of the XVIth Century : the «Burial of Count Orgaz».

Before turning the corner to enter the church, we shall see an old crucifix hanging on the wall; one of the many erected in the XVIIIth Century in the streets of Toledo.

« Burial of the Conde de Orgaz » (painted 1583)

A larger slab under this, one of Greco's most famous pictures, tells us of that pious and generous nobleman being buried in that very site in 1312 and that « St. Agustin and St. Stephen descended from heaven to bury him with their own hands ». Upon his death he had left considerable sums for the poor of that parish and for the upkeep of the church, which he had restored in his life-time — but this will being contested by other heirs to the fortune, a law-suit ensued which lasted 274 years, at the end of which time, the suit was decided in favor of the church. At that time the Greco had made a name for himself and the parish priest entrusted him with painting a picture which would do honour to the dead Count and describe the circumstances which, according to tradition, had occurred at his burial.

This picture is remarkable for its masterful composition, for its superb colouring and the fantasy displayed. Greco painted the principal figure in knight's armour and the two saints that carry the dead body in magnificent church vestments, attended by a young boy (Greco's own son).

It is curious note that on the corner of the handkerchief protruding from the boy's pocket « Greco» has signed his name — DOMENICO THEOTOKOPOULI — and the date (1583).

Three monks of different Religious Orders close the foreground of the picture on the left. To the right, a priest in a transparent white garment over black seems to comment upon the scene and next to him the curate reads from an open book in his hands.

In the long row of mourners are supposedly portrayed friends of Greco's: men of renown of the time such as Cervantes, Lope de Vega, the brothers Covarrubias, the painter Tristan, Greco himself... All the countenances with their depth of expression and smoldering eyes, are solemn, intent; yet each is a magnificent, strikingly individual portrait.

Above soar clouds ridden by small angels. A larger one, the bearer of the Count's soul, pierces the clouds to reach heaven and present the Soul to the Virgin Mary and to St. John the Baptist, at each side of the throne of the Almighly which is surmouted by the Holy Ghost. St. Peter, keys in hand, and many other figures, can be discerned (among them that of Philip II, though still living).

In this, the upper part of the picture, the painter's fantasy runs riot; colours and drawing show some influence of Tintoretto (that artist whom Greco admired most among the Italian painters of the time). The picture, too, evidently proclaims Greco's Byzantine schooling in his beginnings, yet, as a whole, it is typical of the powerful, original style he created and which — consciously or unconciously — has influenced later masters of the Spanish School.

This magnificent work of art, one of Greco's most interesting canvasses, strongly brings out the austere, spiritualized personality, the mastery of colouring, technique and composition — seldom equalled, never surpassed — which have made this genius immortal.

The Palace of the Counts of Fuensalida

As we come out of the church of Santo Tomé we shall continue the same path as before and upon turning the corner, we shall see a superb building with a gothic porch. It is the Palace of the Counts of Fuensalida. In one if its rooms died the Empress Isabella, wife of Charles V and mother of Fhilip II. The removal of the body to Granada incidentally caused the conversion of the Duke of Gandía (San Francisco de Borja), who was profoundly impressed by the decomposition of the dead queen, so recently full of beauty, power and majesty.

* * *

Promenade of St. Christopher

Continuing on our way close to the walls of this palace we arrive at the *Promenade of St. Christopher*, a high and broad natural terrace which offers us a magnificent panoramic view.

In front of us are the green hills which run down steeply toward the river. Between the dark green of the olive groves are to be seen some graceful white houses: the typical « *cigarrales* ». The picturesque hermitage to our left is that of the Virgin of the Valley.

Behind us is the ancient suburb of *Montichel*, where once was the palace of Amru the bloodthisty Moorish King who made sadly famous the « Noche Toledana» (Toledan Night) when, according to tradition, in vengeance, he cut the throats of four hundred Toledan nobles whom he had invited to feast with him.

Further on, Greco's house presents us with the vision of a well kept garden, with the open mouths of some mysterious caves and of a courtyard full of memories.

Nearby we see the Synagogue of Samuel Levy, now known as of « the Tránsito», and in the distance, the Bridge of St. Martin.

The « Cigarrales »

These country-houses are thus called, it is said because of the many crickets *(cigarras)* of which the sloping bank of the river is full. Once inhabited by hermits, these « *Cigarrales* » are now private summer resorts.

Synagogue of Samuel Levy (1365) Later

Monastery of St. Benito, **Now « Tránsito »**

It is a rectangular Hall of large proportions, built during the reign of King Pedro 1 (the Cruel), by his Treasurer and Minister of Finance Samuel Levy, a wealthy and powerful Jew.

Constructed of fine brickwork, its appearance is simple from the outside, constracting strongly with the elaborate inside of fine, handcarved very hard stucco.

It is probably the best Mudejar work in Toledo.

The eastern wall, which receives more intensely the light, is of great beauty on account of its orles and its skirtings. It is a veritable orgy of filigree, of lace-work, of rich embroidery in stucco. Three arches are to be seen — the one in the middle pointed, the others of horse-shoe shape — forming a kind of shallow alcove where the Scriptures were read to the Community by the Doctors of the Law.

The cornice all around is underlined by a long Hebrew inscription containing verses from the Psalms. Under it are several fine marble columns in colour, arranged in pairs, which support a series of arches.

Along the two side walls underneath these arches, runs a superb frieze between two more inscriptions. A kind of intertwined ribbon encloses more verses of the Psalms; here and there are to be seen shields encased in garlands of artistic foliage.

There are, in addition, several *ajimeces* (Moorish windows) carved with great care.

The panelling, of larch wood, the same as that of the reredos of the High Altar of the Cathedral, is carved in geometric figures of great beauty and has the same lovely molding.

High up on the southern wall, are galleries, where the Jewish women used to sit to pray and listen to the readings of the Rabbis.

To this Synagogue was added the plateresque porch when, taken over for Christian worship, it was given to the Monks of St. Benedict (San Benito) and was then, given that appellation.

Later still it was turned over to the Knights of Calatrava, some of whom are buried here, as can be seen from the tombstones and is, since then, known as « El Transito ».

Greco's House

On emerging from the Synagogue of the « Transito », we will go to the house in which the famous artist from Crete, where he was born in 1540, his said to have lived and worked for so many years.

Its door is a little further along the same street. Our attention will be attracted by a pretty courtyard, a very typical kitchen, a room furnished in the style of the period in which the « Greco » lived, and a number of pictures of great value among which are St. Francis by Greco, a copy of Tintoretto, «Washing of the Feet», the Martyrdom of St. Stephen (Spanish School), three Apostles, « A lady » (German School), Mary Magdalene (unknown author), Don Juan of Austria, King Philip II, atributted to Greco; also three paintings on wood, of the XIVth Century.

Passing through the typical charming kitchen, we go into the garden. Some simple columns support a beautiful terrace.

The pallid white of these columns is covered with ivy which climbs up to the balustrade.

Under our feet is the hollow of some dark caves, which give an impression of mystery. Here a former owner of the house, the Marquis of Villena, probably held his famous school of magic. The uneducated must have looked with terror at the mouths of these caves, unaware that this « magic » was nothing but the rudimentary chemistry in which the famed Marquis was so interested.

On the upper floor in a room *supposed* to have been Greco's studio, stands a beautiful canvas by the artist: St. Peter; also a Bassano; a painting representing Greco's hand; a portrait of Queen Isabella II, by an unknown author. In other rooms, St. Francis and a portrait of Don Antonio de Covarrubias by Greco, St. Nicholas of Carvajal, King Philip III by an unknown artist and a painting on wood by Juan de Juanes; the Spolliation of Our Lord (XIIIth Century), The Burial of Our Lord by Bassano; Christ Crucified, by Greco; St. Dominik, by Luis Tristan (a pupil of Greco) and the Bishop Don Diego de Covarrubias, attributed to Greco. Also, King Louis of France, by Greco; a copy of a large picture representing Greco's family (?). St. Francis, by Blas Muñoz, «The Wood-cutters» by Bassano, and others.

* * *

So many and so various are the versions about this so-called «house of Greco» that we have found it fit to add to these lines a clear stating of facts. Fantasy and poor information makes some *see* in every corner the most intimate details of the great painter's life; while others go as far as to even deny that he ever lived in Toledo at all.

There is no doubt whatever that this artist actually lived in Toledo the greater part of is life, as official documents in the archives of this town clearly show. These tell too, of Greco's renting lodgings, the description of which would coincide with the very site of the former Palace of Samuel Levy, of so many vicissitudes (see Note [1], below), and with the description given by the painter Pacheco, Velazquez's father-in-law, who visited El Greco is his last years and left us many details of his abode and mode of working and of living.

Deductions of competent persons based on these informations and on historical facts [1] would go to prove that Greco, when still in his youth, deciding to remain in Toledo, rented and restored part of the former Palace of Samuel Levy, then in ruins, and lived there until his death in 1614. Leaving nothing but debts, his son, the architect Jorge Manuel probably gave it up.

Certain is that the place was in utter ruins and gypsies living in its caves when, at the end of the last century, the Marqués de la Vega Inclán, a great philantropist and admirer of Greco's *reconstructed it in the style of the period*, dedicating to the project great love, artistic taste and intelligence and generously donating it to the nation.

---

(1) NOTE. — This palace, taken from S. Levy when falling into disfavour, was given to supporters of the new Trastamara Dynasty and was inhabited, among others, by the famous « nigromancer » Marquis of Villena and lastly by Count Benavente, who set fire to it himself after his Sovereign, Charles V, had forced him to give hospitality in it to the Connetable de Bourbon, a Frenchman whom the proud Spanish Count considered to be a traitor and his Palace being polluted by Bourbon's presence.

Greco Museum

It is in the same building as the former. Here are kept some very notable pictures by the famous painter. Amongst others «A View and Map of Toledo», «Portrait of the Archbishop Covarrubias», of « B. M. John of Avila»; « Jesus Blessing », « St. John the Evangelist », an «Apostolado» (each one of the twelve Apostles separate) similar to that in the Sacristy of the Cathedral and, in a chapel with a beautiful Moorish ceiling, Greco's magnificent and gripping « St. Bernardino».

St. Mary «The White »
XIIth - XIIIth Centuries (?)

On leaving the Greco Museum and turning the corner of the «Transito » an inscription, not very far away, informs us of the presence of this building which was formerly the *Chief Jewish Synagogue*. Some stone steps lead up to an old door and a small, secluded garden surrouding it.

It is situated in the middle of the Jewish Quarter (or Ghetto), the suburb in which the Jews lived until they were expelled from Spain, shortly after the Conquest of Granada, the ending of the Cathedral and the discovery of America (1492). It is much older than the Synagogue of the « Transito » and was probably constructed a century, or perhaps even two centuries earlier-it is not possible to say. It was dedicated to the Hebrew rite until 1405 when St. Vincent Ferrer, at the head of the exalted multitudes of the church of *Santiago del Arrabal*, threw the Jews out of their Synagogue and turned it into a place for Christian worship.

This Synagegue composed of five naves, is, in its architectural aspect, completely different from that of the « Transito », which looks more like the great hall of a luxurious palace while this of « Santa María », in pure Arab style, looks more like a Mosque.

The octagonal columns, serving as stems to the beautiful capitals, in the composition of which oriental pine-cones are to be seen, are really delightful. So, too, are the horse-shoe arches of a very pure Arabic style, each surmounted by a pair of columns.

All the capitels are different and equally beautiful. Delightful too are those medallions the interiors of which look like lace-work made with supreme delicacy by skilful hands.

In 1550 it became a hostel for repentant fallen women and later still it was dedicated to a hermitage under the patronage of St. Mary called by the people «The White One», after the chapel of that same appellation in Rome.

School of Arts and Crafts

(Escuela de Artes y Oficios)

Further along the road we see a large modern building the predominating styles of wich are the Mudejar and Gothic, in the construction of which only brick, iron and tiles have been employed.

It is the School of Arts and Crafts. In it workers and persons who wish it are taught taste and perfection in these specialties.

The principal façade exhibits a shield of Ferdinand and Isabella (a yoke and a bunch of arrows), pages and kings-at-arms.

* * *

Close by is the universally famous Monastery of St. John of the Kings.

St. John of the Kings
(End of XVth Century)

This marvel of late Gothic architecture is, in its style, one of the most remarkable in the world. We are taken back to the glory of the genial architect, Juan Guas, the artist who conceived this masterpiece, consisting of Church, Cloister and Monastery.

The entrance to the Church, however, is the work of of Alfonso de Covarrubias, celebrated architect of the XVIth Century.

Hanging on the outside wall are the heavy chains of the Christian prisoners whom the « Catholic Kings » freed from Moorish slavery. Many a sad tale would these chains tell us, were they to speak.

Queen Isabella and King Ferdinand, the «Catholic Sovereigns» had this sumptuous building made, at their own private expense, as thanksgiving for the victory at the Battle of Toro (1476), a victory that assured the Crown of Castille for Isabella. This right to the Crown was being conteded by her niece Joan, nicknamed « La Beltraneja », whom the Portuguese King was upholding. This battle of great historical importance was, in fact, the turning-point in Spain's history : the beginning of her Golden Age.

Upon entering the Church we are impressed by its loftiness, its beautiful proportions and its exquisite workmanship, the superb beauty of its pillars lavishly and delicately ornamented, the cornice all around the wall, flowing gracefully into two pews of beautifully chiselled open-work stone balustrade, in their centre the interwoven initials of Ferdinand and Isabella. The slender, elegant pillars rise still further above, finishing off in fanciful chapitels of leaves and heads. On these pillars rest strong, elegant, ample arches forming the base for a large horizontal ring, from which the great vault springs that generously lets in the light.

Nearing the high altar, on both sides of the church, great eagles support huge scutcheons with the emblems of the different realms brought together by Isabella (Castille and Loon) and Ferdinand (Aragon, Catalonia and Naples). Thus was wrought the unity of Spain which, together with her discovery of America, made her mistress of the world.

This magnificent church was intended to be the burial place of the King and Queen who had had it built; however; they were buried in the Cathedral in Granada.

During the invasión by Napoleon's troops (1810) this church suffered much, having been turned into a stable by the invaders.

It is now being repaired.

To the Monastery adjouning is linked the name of its first novice : the great *Cardinal Cisneros* (See p. 68).

From the church, through a beautiful door on the right we pass straight on to the Cloister and Courtyard.

Cloister of St. John of the Kings

Beautiful as the Church is, the Cloister even surpasses it. It is universally considered as a model of late of «florid» Gothic style, with all its wonderful filigree stonework,—that Gothic about to die, crushed by its own finished perfection. There is no school of Art but possesses reproductions of this magnifcent work. Upon entering it, one is deeply impressed by the richness of its dazzling white stone carvings, its great beauty of proportion and its play of light — specially on sunlit days.

Each pillar, surmounted by an almost life-sized beautiful statue is lavishly decorated with foliage, animals, figures — grotesque and otherwise — monster, etc. ... everything imaginable turned into delicate decorative motives, in constant variation. At the height of the chapitels, a magnificent frieze goes all around.

The four interior walls are pierced by huge Gothic windows of most exquisite open-work stone forming a luxurious frame to a courtyard full of verdure.

The charm of this spot, secluded, dreamy, evoquing memories will not readily fade from our thoughts.

A magnificent plateresque staircase, the work of Covarrubias, leads to the upper gallery just above, the ceiling of beautifully carved woodwork.

Cambron Gate (XVth Century)

This gate formed part of the walls built by the Visigothic King Wamb in the VIIth Century and later repaired by Alphonso VI in the XIIth.

In 1575 it was restored, in grecorroman style, as its half pointed arches, its triangular pyramids, its doric columns denote. Those outside are Arabic.

In this part is a great shield bearing the royal arms.

The last restoration was probably made some twenty years after that of the New Visahra Gate, in the reign of Philip II.

Partly destroyed during the late civil war (1936); it has now been again repaired.

Panoramic view

On passing the Cambron Gate one can enjoy one of the most beautiful panoramic views which this « Imperial » City has to offer.

Leaving on our right the statues of the Gothic Kings Sisebuto and Sisenando, we advance to the end of the splendid terrace. At our feet the most fertile «vega» (plain), of exhuberant green, spreads to the amphitheatre of grey hills which loom far off on the horizon.

The Tagus, tame once more after passing the Bridge of St. Martin, flows peacefully on. From here we also see the Basilica de Santa Leocadia (see p. 85) and further on some great red-roofed pavilions which stand out amongst the leafy green of the trees : the famed NATIONAL ARMS FACTORY.

National Arms Factory (XVIIIth Century)

From time immemorial, TOLEDO - STEEL has been famous : the waters of the Tagus being supposed to have special properties for the tempering of this metal.

This industry used to be scattered about the town but Charles III founded this factory (1780) on the banks of the river and the outskirts of the city where it could spread out and do its work more efficiently. It mainly provided warfare material, but nowadays instruments for clinics and laboratories are also being made and, as well, « damaskeened » work and many marvels in hammered metal.

Basilica St. Leocadia
or Christ of the Plain
(Cristo de la Vega)

Going down the hill to the Basica of St. Leocadia, passing through a courtyard with flowers and some straight tall cypresses we enter the famous basilica erected about 606 by the Gothic King Sisebuto in the same place where Santa Leocadia, a Toledan martyr, was buried.

The ancient Basilica was destroyed by Moorish fanaticism when the Sarecens arrived in Toledo a century later and was after re-erected in the Mudejar style using part of the material of the original.

This basilica is famous too, because in it were held many of the first Councils of the early Church, also for being the pantheon of several Gothic kings; of St. Eugene, first Bishop of Toledo successor it is said, of St. Peter; of St. Eladio, St. Julian... and others.

Here, too, is where — according to tradition — St. Leocadia appeared to St. Ildephonse and to King Recesvinto in the year 666. Lastly it is famous, because of the romantic legend of love inmortalized by the poet Zorrilla.

A modern monument to the Heart of Jesus guards it at present.

On leaving the hermitage, and following the banks of the river in the direction of the *Bridge of St. Martin*, we shall arrive at the ancient keep known by the name of *The Bath of « La Cava »*.

The Bath of « La Cava » (Baño de la Cava)

It was probebly the entrance to the bridge which the Romans constructed and which was destroyed by a great flood of the Tagus, some years after a similar one which destroyed the Bridge of Alcantara.

This keep is known by the poetic name of the *Baño de la Cava* because, according to the legend, it was in this place that the beautiful Florinda daughter of Count Julian used to bathe and that Don Rodrigo, the last Gothic king; fell in love with her but, not able to conquer her virtue, he in despair abandoned the affairs of the kingdom already decadent, which finally sank on the banks of the river Guadalete (711).

Another legend will have it that, unable to gain Florinda's favour, the King dishonoured her upon which her father, the faithful count Julian, swore vengeance and, going over to the Moors, lead them against Toledo and its king.

Whether there be or not any foundation to any of the several legend related to this part of Spain's history and whatever was the cause of the downfall of the Visigothic rule in Spain after 300 years of dominion, the fact is that her doors were then opened to the Moors who, appearing before Toledo in 711 stayed on Spanish soil for eight centuries.

Bridge of St. Martin
(reconstructed in XIVth Century)

The Bridge of St. Martin is very similar in its construction to that of Alcantara, so much so that it is believed to have been so built by order of King Alphonse X, the Wise, enamoured of the solidity and beauty of the other bridge.

The bridge of Alcantara has two spans; that of St. Martin five. Like the other; it has one keep at the entrance and another at the exit.

The bridge is of gothic or ogival style. Should we stand on it, we would see, as we did before on the Bridge of Alcantara, the contrast which the river offers upstream and downstream.

It is said that the scuptured head which is to be seen above the keystone of the main arch represents the wife of the architect. (See Legends at end of book p. 96).

This bridge suffered a great deal during the struggle between Peter the Cruel and his half-brother Henry of Trastamara.

It was restored by Archbishop Tenorio, the restorer, too, of the Castle of St. Servando.

On the entrance-keep can be seen a statue of St. Julian, the patron of the bridge, attributed to Berruguete, the cele-brated artist of the sepulchre of Tavera, of the porch of St. Clement, of the upper choir of the Cathedral...

At the exit of the bridge exists a great statue representing Alphonse VII, the Emperor, he who gave Toledo, as a coat-of-arms, two seated kings It can be seen on the keep which is nearest to the city.

* * *

Retracing our steps and leaving the Basilica on our left we follow the highway bordering the fortifications and, at some distance down in the « Vega » (plain), the faint remains of Roman buildings are to be discerned.

The Old Visagra Gate

Puerta Antigua de Visagra (Xth Century)

This Gate is also called of Ālphons VI, because through it this King entered with the Cid Campeador at the head of his Christian troops in 1085, when he reconquered the city, in Moorish hands since 711.

This gate has often needed reconstructions and only part of the original structure is left, but through it all its original character has been kept.

It is of pure Ārab construction as can be seen by its horseshoe arches, the columns on which the outer ones are supported, the battlements of the tower and the construction of the walls, which is similar to that of the church of Santiago del Ārrabal.

Passing through this old gate we shall be following the same path which the triumphant Christian army probably followed, arriving along steep streets at the Moorish mosque known as the Christ of Light (p. 24 to 26), subsequently reaching the centre of the town.

If, however, we follow on along the road bordering the embattlements, we shall come to the *New Visagra Gate* close by.

Roman Remains B. C. 193 - A. D. 200

Evidently Toledo, the capital of Carpetania and, during Roman, rule the principal city of their «Colonia» on the Iberian Peninsula, had here had its large building; but only slight traces of the remain. There is, however, a well-founded belief that the ruins of the amphiteatre (a semicircular enclosure of stone and mortar about 3 ft. thick, of varying height) and an arch, belonging to Roman Circus, a place reserved for the spectables which delighted the ancient Romans, date from that time.

Some other remains are to be seen in the city itself: the so-called «Hercules Cave» of the legends — probably the crypt of a Jupiter Temple — and a fragment of a once-important aqueduct near the Bridge of Alcantara.

Palace of Cardinal Lorenzana (XVIIIth Century)

Following on the same road and direction we find, built into the very fortifications, at its foot a sunken garden, the Palace of the learned Cardinal Lorenzana, the founder of the « Instituto » (college) in the Square of St. Vicente.

It has lately been turned into a Hotel or « Hostal ».

* * *

Through the Streets of Toledo typical nooks

Many are the picturesque streets and «patios» (courtyards) of this old city and many the buildings full of history and histories. Almost everywhere bright-coloured flowers lighten up the sombre stones.

South of the Cathedral are the street named «of the Bitter Well» (Pozo Amargo) of the well-known legend (see p. 96); the street of Sta. Isabel with the XVIth Century Convent of that same name with its mudejar apses of typical construction of brick and stone, and a handsome gothic porch.

In the middle of the square in front of this Convent are the remains of the Palace of King Pedro I « the Cruel » in its time a nest of intrigue.

The most notable part of this structure is the porch in mudejar style from which project the lovely coving and the wellcarved pinewood beams which sustain it. At the present time the building houses a school.

North of the Cathedral, at some distance away from it and not far from the mosque of the « Christ of Light », we shall find the places of interest which follow :

Towards Santo Domingo el Real (XIVth Century)

Climbing a very steep street and then turning to the right we arrive at the Square of the Carmelitas Descalzos, the porch of its church in Greco-roman style.

Continuing on our journey between the high wall of ancient convent; we stand before the entrance of the famous *Passages (cobertizos) of Santo Domingo el Real* (XVth Century).

Immediately to our left is a short passage in whose walls a «Dolorosa» weeps; further on a lonely street bathed in light; in the back-ground the beautiful silhouette of a Mudejar tower, and in front of us there is a long, narrow passage in almost complete darkness which never receives the sun's rays. Still further on, an enormous cross. At its feet tremulous hands have traced women's names. Then the shadows mingle again with the light.

And now we have arrived at the Square Santo Domingo el Real, called also the «Romantic Square».

The Romantic Square (XIVth Century)

This quiet and solitary square, far removed, is one of the most typical corners of Toledo.

The four Doric columns which sustain the beautiful portico of the church give it a truly charming aspect. . .

In the background is the wall of the Convent, on one side of which is an ancient cross crowned by a small cave.

A white plaque tells of the remembrance of the Toledan students for that sublime poet of sorrowfull love : Gustavo Adolfo Bécquer (1870).

Convent and Square of St. Clara

Retracing our steps and passing the passage, in the left wall of which weeps a «Dolorosa», we turn to the right in order to see the portico of the *Convent of St. Clara*.

Once we have left the *Square of St. Clara*, in which is situated the entrance to the Convent, we pass beind the *National Institute of Secondary Education* (XVIIIth Century), institution of Cardinal Lorenzana (p. 89).

We shall see that in almost all the façades of the private houses of this street specially Nos. 1 and 7, art has left its beautiful traces. The courtyard of the former is very attractive.

It is a beautiful Arab courtyard, of which there are a great number in this marvellous city.

National Institute (XVth Century)

Turning the corner, we face the Institute — which in ancient times was a famous university — its neo-classic façade finished off by a coat of arms of Cardinal Lorenzana, a great protector of the Institute and of everything which represented faith, culture or progress (see p. 89).

Four large jonic colums, the capitels of which are in the form of a C face downwards — like those of the Hospital of Tavera and of the Provincial Asylum — adorn it.

On both sides, in great niches, there are excellent statues which represent the Sciences.

* * *

Stone steps outside this building lead down to the Square of St. Vincent where the church of lhe same name — now a Museum — stands.

The Square of Padilla
(Plazuela de Padilla)

In this square existed formerly the house of Juan de Padilla, the punctilious Toledan who, seeing the liberties of the Castillians threatened by the decrees of Charles V, fought and died in their defence.

So fiercely did he fight for these liberties that the anger of the Emperor caused him to order that the house of the brave Toledan should be destroyed and its site sown with salt, so that «the grass soud never again grow in that place». To-day it is one of the most solitary and quiet corners of the city.

The House of Garcilaso de la Vega

(XVIth Century)

Continuing on our way, descending several steps and turning to the right, an inscription in deep black letters on brilliant white back-ground tells that this is the site of the manorial house of *the valiant warrior and sweet poet* of Toledo, *Garcilaso de la Vega*, who was born almost at the time as the great Queen Isabella died.

The house of Garcilaso had the honour of entertaining King Ferdinand and Queen Isabella when they came to Toledo to marry their daughter Isabella to the King of Portugal, the latter receiving hospitality in the house of Padilla.

It was in that house that the batallion of Toledan students was organised which, under the patronage of the *Virgen del Sagrario*, actuated by a noble and exalted feeling of patriotism and faith, went during the War of Independence (1808-1810) to Cadiz to fight for the honour of the country.

This batallion of Toledan students bore itself so bravely that it served later as a nucleus from which was formed the Infantry Academy, still existant in Toledo.

The Tower of St. Roman (Xth Century)

Returning to the Square of Padilla and the Street of Esteban Illan, we will continue our journey down the short, dark and solitary street, the first on the right. A tower built on the loftiest part of the city surprises us with its strength, its gracefulness and its arrogance. It has the beautiful aspect lent to it by Arab style and is proud of the part it has played in history. In 1166 it had the honour of serving as royal residence in a troubled hour.

In its topmost storey adorned with tapestries and damasks, King Alphonso VIII — the future victor of the Navas de Tolosa — slept one sultry night in the month of August. The following morning, when the light of dawn entered the room in which the boy-king slept, the purple banner of Castille appeared through the horse-shoe arches. And the powerful and firm voice of the famous Toledan. Esteban Illan, proclaimed little Alphons as its Sovereign to the cheers of the multitude below, which acclaimed the new Monarch.

The Gateway and Asylum of St. Clement
(XVIth Century)

Taking the solitary street to the right, we come up to this beautiful, richly adorned, plateresque doorway due to the famous Berruguete, the artist who carved the tomb of Cardinal Tavera and the stall on the left side of the Choir of the Cathedral.

Proceeding on our tour we shall pass the greco-roman doorway of the church of St. Peter Martyr and, on **turning** the corner, we shall come to a small quiet square with some trees — the Square of Juan de Mariana.

Above the grey roofs soars the pointed tower of the Cathedral. On the opposite side of the square, broad stone steps lead up to an imposing brick mass: the Church of St. Ildephons, better known as the «Jesuit Church» of St. John.

Not far from here is another small square : that of Amador de los Ríos, its railings enclosing a few trees.

* * *

We are now passing over a buried *via Romana* (Roman road) which had its entrance, it is said, in the now inaccessible Cave of Hercules, behind a wall in the nearby lane of St. Gines

Visigothic Remains

We enter the street of St. Ginés at the end of which, in a lane on the left, we find some Visigothic stones built into the wall by the Bridge of Alcantara, and in the Mudejar tower of Santo Tomé.

Passing through the street of the Brothers Becquer and of Santa Justa, with its lovely horse-shoe arch, which formerly gave entrance to the then Mozarabic church of that name, we end our tour, again quite near the Square of Zocodover.

* * *

OLD LEGENDS OF TOLEDO

Notes on Toledo would be incomplete without a mention of its legends, some of which have been inserted into the text of this bookle (pp. 27, 28, 86).

To these we shall here add a couple of the most popular ones :

The legend of the Bridge of St. Martin

Says that when the architect was finishing it, he became aware of great error he had made and, certain that when the scaffolding were taken away, the bridge would collapse, he fell ill with anxiety. His wife, in order to cover up his mistake, set fire to the woodwork during the night and the bridge fell in.

The architect then corrected his plans, made a new, solid construction and no one discovered his first error, believing the fire to have been accidental.

The legend further says that the sculptured head over the central arch of the structure is suposed to be the portrait of that wife who so boldly saved her husband's professional reputation.

Legend of « The Bitter Well »
(Pozo Amargo)

The Street of *The Bitter Well* (Pozo Amargo) so named after the legend, starts from the southern corner of the Town Hall Square, near the Cathedral. This legend is one of the many existing in Toledo relative to Christians and Jews the latter having been very powerful in this town for many years.

Rachel, a beautiful Hebrew maiden, fell in love with a Christian knight who sang his love to her under her « ajimez » (window), braving the hatred between races and religions. But one night a treacherous dagger (the story says it was that of Levi, her own father) ended the knight's song and life. His body was thrown into the well of the house and, eve after, Rachel's tears fiowed into the well turning water bitter.

Legend of « The Stream of the Beheaded Woman »

(Arroyo de la Degollada)

The legend of *The Stream of the Beheaded Woman* (Arroyo de la Degollada) is another tragic one with a similar motif.

A lavely Jewish maid lived with her father on the opposite bank of the river. A Christian student, deeply in love with her, used to cross the river to visit her. The wicked father who had observed their secret meetings, one night put an end to the youth's life and beheaded his lovely daughter. Carrying her head all the way down the hill, he threw it into the stream below. Every drop of blood, as it fell on the ground, turned into a bright red pebble, and that is how that hill came to be strewn with the half- precious stones known as «granats».

It is a fact that many such stones were formerly to be found on this hill-side which slopes down to the Circum- venting Road at the point where a modern viaduct crosses the valley.

Legend of the Christ of the Plain

(Cristo de la Vega)

This is one of the best known legends.

In the time of Philip II, it tells, the beautiful Inés de Vargas and her lover, the gallant captain Diego Martínez were to part. Diego was to go to war in far away lands and gain honours and triumphs before marrying her. On one of their walks before his departure they reached an old silent hermitage in the broad plain to the west of the city and Inés made Diego promise eternal love before the image of Christ crucified which was on the altar.

Time passed and Diego, returning from far away lands loaded with glory, scorned the faithful Inés. No one recognized her rights when the grief-stricken maiden invoked the justice of men. There had been no witness to the vows of love...

Inés, then remembered the only witness pressent : that Christ hanging, suffering and abandoned on the Cross and, exalted by a mystic fervor, she gave the Divine Name to the judge.

The judge, surrounded by the multitude gathered at the hermitage, opened the Gospels near the divine breast asking repeatedly, in the name of human justice, if He had been witness to the vow. When, for the third time the judge put the question, one of the hands of the Christ solemnly came down on the Gospels and the words « I swear » were clearly heard from the divine lips.

The crowd fell on its knees; Diego rushed towards the abandoned Inés; the bell tolled happily and so it tolls on century after century, from Easter to Whitsun, calling the Toledan couples to the poetical festival of love.

This figure of Christ crucified, one arm hanging by its side, is to be seen in the hermitage of the «Christ of the Plain» or Basilica of S. Leocadia (pag. 85) to this day.

Legend of « The Little Pins »

(Alfileritos)

Not far from Zocodover Square and ending in that of St. Vincent is a long narrow street which takes its name from this legend. In a recess in one of the walls, an iron gate before it, is a charming little shrine with a statuette of the Virgin Mary, pins strewn at her feet.

The story tells that long, long ago there was a lovely Toledo maid who had a deep devotion to this particular effigy and when her lover went to the war she prayed hours and hours before it, that his life might be saved and that he would return safe. But as during her long, nightly vigils at the shrine she often fell asleep, she told the old «duenna» who used to accompany her that whenever this happened she was to wake her up by pricking her with a pin. Every time the pin had to be used she would afterwards push it through the grating at the feet of the Virgin as a contrite offering for not having kept constant watch.

Great was the rejoicing when the lover returned safe and true and to this day many young girls throw in their pin-offering asking the «Virgin of Ālfileritos» for protection.

FAREWELL TO TOLEDO

Traveller, who has seen the splendid monuments that tell of Toledo's past glory keep the remembrance in your heart of this city where Spain's greatness was tempered — like Toledo steel — at the anvil of hard sufferings and courage; were the bold venture of Columbus found hearing and support, thus giving un the New World; and where that world-renowned, restless spirit known as «El Greco», having in vain sought in Crete, Greece and Rome the inner harmony with his surroundings which his tormented soul yearned for found it, at last, in Toledo.

E N D

INDEX

* These are to be found the text of the book.

FOR ORDERS
APPLY TO:

LUIS ARRIBAS

CIUDAD, 1   TOLEDO

General view.

Gate of Bisagra.

Bridge of St. Martin and River Tagus.

Bridge of Alcantara.

Gate of the Sun (XV Cent.).

Façade of St. John of the Kings, illuminated.

Church of St. John of the Kings.

Church of St. John of the Kings.

Cloister of St. John of the Kings.

Cloister of St. John of the Kings.

Cloister of St. John of the Kings.

Holy Mary the White.

Synagogue of the Transition.

St. Thomé. The burial of Count Orgaz (Greco).

Greco's House. The Garden.

Patio of El Greco's house.

El Greco's house. Kitchen.

Museum of El Greco. Studio.

Tears of St. Peter.

Museum of Tavera. Detail of the Holy Family.

Partial view and Alcazar.

The Alcazar. Monument to the Angel of Victory.

Bridge of Alcantara and the Alcazar.

Museum of the Holy Cross.

Museum of the Holy Cross. Staircase.

Museum of the Holy Cross.

Museum of the Holy Cross. The Assumption (Greco).

Museum of the Holy Cross. The Crowning of the Virgin (Greco).

General view.

Cathedral with illuminations.

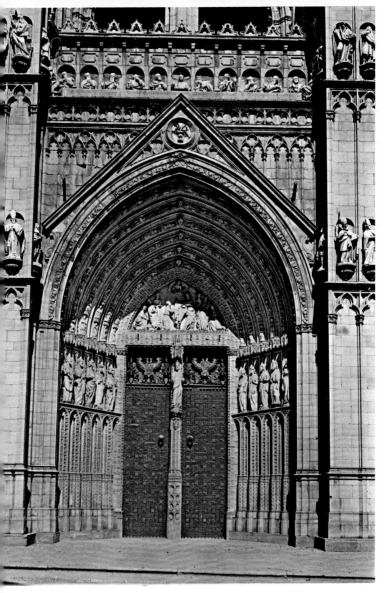

Cathedral. Main door.

Cathedral. Retable of the High Altar.

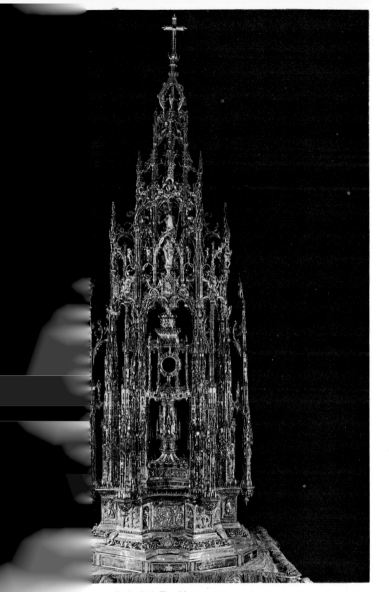

Cathedral. The Monstrance.

Cathedral. The Choir.

Cathedral. White Virgin.

Cathedral. The Transparente.

Cathedral. Organ and Door of the Emperor.

Cathedral. Capitulary room.

Cathedral. Central Nave. Choir and high retable.

Sagrada Familia (Van Dyck)

Cathedral. Virgin of the Tabernacle.

Cathedral. St. Francis of Assisi.

Spolliation of Christ.

Bridge of St. Martin and Partial view.

Bridge of Alcántara and the Alcázar.

Street of St. Elizabeth.

Typical Toledan vendor.